The Power of Dreams
How to Access Creative Ideas & Innovative Solutions

Gary K. Yamamoto

Cypress Mountain Books
An Imprint of Dynamic Pathways, Inc.
Tucson, Arizona

THE POWER OF DREAMS
Copyright © 2022 Gary K. Yamamoto

Library of Congress Control Number: 2021925564

ISBN: 9781878182043 (eBook)
ISBN: 9781878182050 (paperback)

Contents

Preface v

Introduction vii

1: Power Dreaming...1

2: The Making of a Dream Expert...7

3: Five Types of Dreams 15

4: Success Dreams for Authors 25

5: Success Dreams For Lottery Winners...31

6: Success Dreams for Businesses and Inventors 37

7: Success Dreams for Scientists and Mathematicians 43

8: Success Dreams for Entertainers 47

9: Success Dreams for Medical Personnel 51

10: Success Dreams for Artists...52

11: Success Dreams for Psychics..55

12: Miscellaneous Success Dreams 59

13: Developing a Creative Mindset..63

14: Get The Dreams You Want 73

15: Your Dream Log..81

16: Extracting the Dream Messages 87

17: Building a Business from Your Dreams 91

18: Your Dream Adventure 101

Supplement: History of Dream Analysis..103

About the Author 105

Dedication

Andrea Gold whose faith and support helped to get this book completed and published.

William Buehler showed me the true potential found in dreams.

Patricia Rochelle Diegel urged me to continue with dream because they were an important means to open people's minds to possibilities.

Bill Southwood, who gave me unbelievable support and predicted I had a second dream book to write.

Barry Wishner urgently called to say he dreamed the title of my book, The Power of Dreams.

Preface

In times of rapid change, life can become difficult. Artificial intelligence and machines are replacing jobs. Natural disasters, including forest fires, hurricanes, global warming, earthquakes, and tsunamis, destroy homes and businesses. Every day, you face difficulties and problems rising from government and business changes created by a pandemic and the need to work remotely. You need to have an advantage to excel in this challenging environment.

As an electrical engineer, I've worked in communication and nuclear weapons. I found that engineering was nothing more than a series of problems I had to solve. Fortunately, my dreams proved to be invaluable. They gave me ideas and helped me to solve problems. They were there to provide guidance and offer critical insights. I knew I was not alone in using my dreams to help me through life. With the search capability of Google, I found so many others who had benefited from their dreams. It shocked me to see how many willingly admitted that their insights, inventions, and realizations came from their dreams. Many others may have found ideas and solutions while taking a shower or driving to work. I believe it's that quiet time when a person understands the message in their latest dreams.

My engineering background has trained me to use what works and discard what doesn't. I've found that dreams work! They can not only help you at work but also guide you through all your personal situations and relationships. They will even guide you when it's time to leave your job for another. They may also guide you to discover your soul mate or tell you it's time to end a relationship that's not working.

So I set out to write a second book on dreams. This book focuses on using your dreams to unlock your full potential. This was a relatively challenging book for me to write. This is my 13th major revision. It's been an amazing evolutionary process. As I reviewed each version, it presented a new idea or approach, often flowing out in my dreams. Each made the message of this book clearer and more useful. This all took place in 12 months during the COVID-19 pandemic. You'll find this book very useful in helping you unleash your creativity and open up possibilities.

Introduction

In a world filled with billions of people, why is it that only a few make it to the top? What was it that made them so different that they were honored with great accolades and tremendous wealth? If you look at them carefully, they didn't do dozens of wonderful things or invent a hundred powerful tools. From what I found, they had one or two great ideas. They expanded on their idea and added more ideas and solutions later. The constant process of adding new ideas and solutions gained them fame and/or fortune.

Thomas Edison may have had a thousand patents, but we primarily remember him for the electric light. Albert Einstein may have been a genius, but you probably know him for the Theory of Relativity. These two giants of innovation received their inspiration from their dreams.

This morning, you may have had such a dream. If you were working on a problem at work, the dream you recalled as you opened your eyes may have been the solution you needed. Unfortunately, if you had an alarm ringing and the need to use the bathroom, or children running around, you immediately forgot your dream. Fortunately, if you took a quiet shower or silently drove alone to work, you may recall that idea or solution. You may not realize that the solution initially came from your dream.

In our rapidly evolving and changing world, the need to have significant creative ideas and innovative solutions increases. A significant idea is not simply changing the color of a product or the shape of the grill in a car. It's the ideas that created the nuclear reactor and Google. It put a man on the moon and created unique artists like Salvador Dali. Then there are powerful authors, including Stephenie Meyer and Stephen King, who benefited from their dreams.

I realized people aren't that interested in creativity and innovation. Instead, they're interested in creating something new, something that can change the way we communicate and even how we live. My hope is for you to benefit from your dreams each time you fall asleep. To make the most of your time sleeping, you'll program yourself before bed to gain the dreams you need. As you make use of and benefit from your dreams, please drop me a line to let me know how it's working out for you. You can get more information on: dynamicpathways.com.

Chapter 1
Power Dreaming

Dreams come true. Without that possibility, nature would not incite us to have them.

— John Updike

You had a dream last night. You may or may not remember it when you got up, but you had at least one dream! It may have been a simple dream, repeating something memorable you did the day before. Or, it could also have been a message that's trying to save your life or provide you with an idea that could lead you to fame and fortune. Here are a few examples of what your dreams may have been trying to convey to you.

Lifesaving Dreams

Eugene Daly boarded the Titanic as a young man traveling in steerage. Every day, he told his friend, Bertha Mulvihill, his repeating dreams the ship was going to sink. Once onboard, he continued to have more dreams of the ship sinking. On Sunday, he told everyone he met the ship would sink that night. Just as he predicted, the ship hit an iceberg. Fortunately, because he and Bertha knew the ship was going to sink, they were both saved. He lived to tell of how his dreams had saved their lives.

If you had a similar series of dreams of a tragedy, what would you do? Would you have seen it as just another dream and disregarded it? Or would you think it was a lot of nervous energy about your upcoming adventure and taken the trip, anyway? Or would you have seen it as a warning of sorts and postponed or canceled the trip?

Future Event Dreams

In 1858, Mark Twain worked with his brother on the steamboat, Pennsylvania. One night in St. Louis, he had a dream where his brother lay dead in a metal coffin in the living room. It was so clear and vivid and could see in great detail what his brother had on. When he woke up, he was sure his brother was dead. Even walking into the living room and finding no coffin, it still took a long walk to convince him it was all a dream.

Two weeks later, Twain traveled with his brother from St. Louis to New Orleans on the riverboat, Pennsylvania. He then left his brother and transferred to another boat. On the return trip, the boilers on the Pennsylvania exploded and badly wounded his brother. When his brother looked as if he was going recovering, he received an overdose of morphine which killed him.

When Twain went to the funeral parlor and saw that his brother was in a metal coffin. His brother wore the clothes Twain had seen in his dream. Although the dream should have prepared Twain for his brother's untimely death, it haunted Twain for the rest of his life.

Music Dreams

In the middle of the night on May 7, 1965, Keith Richards woke up from a dream with a melody in his head. Unfamiliar with the layout of his hotel room in Clearwater, Florida, he searched for his portable cassette recorder. Finding it, he pushed the record button. He then grabbed his guitar on the bed next to him, played a riff along with a vocal, and then fell back asleep.

The next morning, he pushed the record button on the cassette player and it wouldn't run. He initially thought the player was broken. But then, he remembered inserting a new tape the evening before. Looking carefully, he found the cassette was already at the end of the spool. Curiosity caused him to rewind the tape and push play. He heard an eight-note riff along with the vocal line, "I can't get no satisfaction." The next sound was the pick falling and Richards' snoring through the rest of the tape. Of course, his creation still required work. Mick Jagger had to write the lyrics. They had to change the arrangement to transform it from folk to rock.

If you were a budding musician or a member of a new musical group, would it be valuable to be given a hit song while you slept? Would your career and financial success leap forward? It could happen! And if it did, it could change your life and even your fortune.

Lottery Dreams

Mason Krentz of Silver Lake, Kansas, dreamed he won $25,000 in the lottery. Two days later, he bought a 100X scratch-off ticket and another game ticket in Topeka. When he showed only one number match on his ticket, he didn't expect to win much. Then he realized he had won $75,000; three times more than the dream had depicted.

Krentz said he would use the money to get a new vehicle for his wife and purchase a plot of land in Silver Lake. The rest will go into his mutual fund.

If you had a dream of winning a lot of money from the lottery, would you go out and purchase a ticket? Or would you do what Mary Wollens did when she had her winning dream? She was so sure she was going to win; she didn't just go out and buy a single lottery ticket with her numbers. Instead, she got a second ticket with the same numbers. For her efforts, she won 2/3 of the $24 million jackpot prize and took home $16 million.

Business Dreams

Recently, a business owner asked me to interpret his dream at the beginning of a meeting. He said he had the same dream his entire life. This dream found him being chased by a T-Rex dinosaur. He asked me what it meant.

I said being chased by a T-Rex meant that he always wanted to be the top dog. He immediately agreed with that short interpretation. Since we were in a business meeting and sitting with other business owners in the room, I stopped there.

But there was more that he didn't hear. I didn't say he had long been on his quest to become the top dog. In his mind, there was always more for him to accomplish. His repeating T-Rex dream meant his goal was a continually moving target, always rising higher. He was always finding another goal, one that was just a little beyond his reach. As he achieved one goal, he'd unconsciously set another one a little further out, and perhaps a little higher. If he evaluated himself, he would find he had a driver's personality.

I also didn't mention his business personality was like a T-Rex; one which would be glad to eat (purchase) any business he liked (was profitable) and found tasty (reasonably priced). And like the T-Rex, he'll probably continue doing the same thing until he dies. Perhaps this was also true of his personal life, but I didn't delve into it because he gave no more details about his dream or any other dreams he has had. He did mention, if we ever thought of selling our speakers bureau business, he would be interested.

By not using his dream to give him further insights and guidance, he's missing out on so much more. He could have analyzed and interpreted any other dream messages he received between the T-Rex ones. He could have programmed his dreams to allow him to further improve his business and personal lives. He may have received an idea from a dream that would have allowed him to excel far beyond his present goals. It could have been an insight similar to those that have led so many people to fame, fortune, and even saved their lives.

He'll probably tell a few close associates and family members what I said. He may occasionally stop to evaluate his life, but it's my feeling he'll simply continue what he's doing. There's so much more he could do by working with his dreams. He could use his dreams to solve problems and gain deeper insights into the people he hires. He could discover new and creative ideas for business and even in his personal life.

If you were to receive a quick explanation of a dream you had and it sounded accurate, would you wish to learn more? Would you pursue it, even if you were in a place where it would be uncomfortable to discuss your dreams? Or would you consider delving into the meaning of your dreams later? Better yet, would you then look at your dreams for insights, solutions, advice, and ideas?

It's no accident we call our highest aspirations—dreams!

— Gary K. Yamamoto

Your Waking Dream

You probably have at least one waking dream or vision you'd like to achieve inside of you. It may be a single focus on quickly paying off your student debt. Or you may continue to have your childhood dream of achieving fame and fortune. Perhaps your dream is to end world hunger or improve our environment. Whatever it is, your sleeping dreams can help you achieve your aspirational dreams.

You, like everyone else, have been dreaming all your life. Since people have been dreaming for all of recorded history, dreams must serve a purpose. If they didn't, evolution would have faded humankind's dreams into oblivion? Ponder for a moment that your dreams have been working constantly to improve your life?

Changing Your Life

Dreams do several things for you. They are here to give you what you need. It can even provide what you want. Let's see how you can use the most powerful tools of dreams, their ability to give you creative ideas and innovative solutions.

Using Your Dreams for Creative Ideas

- Get new ideas or techniques in art.
- Use dream ideas to create music.
- Have a powerful story to tell and become a novelist.
- Gain insights into the characters or environment in your novel.
- Create a more fulfilling and meaningful life.
- A new method to illustrate a marketing piece or book.
- Experience a lucid dream unleashing your mindset possibilities.

Using Your Dream for Innovative Solutions

- A plan to change an organization's culture.
- A way to improve a business process.
- Create a way to improve customer service.
- Improve marketing and accelerate sales.

Using Your Dreams to Improve Your Personal and Business Life

- Finding your soul mate.
- Have more and better sex dreams.
- Experience an adventure in your dreams.
- Become a recognized expert in your field.

- Just want to be independently wealthy.
- Start your own small business on the side.

If any in the above list interests you, this book will show you how. You'll ask for and receive the dreams you want. If you can't get it, there's always another chance the next night. You can then use them to improve your work and career, along with your personal life.

The True Power of Dreams

Getting a creative idea or an innovative solution is great. But it's not enough. It takes a lot of effort to create a new or unique product or service. There will be additional questions and problems along the way. With dreams, it continues to give you guidance and suggestions. This alone is enough to justify programming your dreams and discovering new solutions.

So have an open mind as you read the stories of the people who have used their dreams to better their lives and even gain fame and fortune. While the examples may seem extreme, there are millions of others who have untold stories of how they benefitted from their dreams. I hope to help you gain whatever you desire. Count yourself as a power dreamer who transformed your life through your dreams.

Chapter 2
The Making of a Dream Expert

Dreams are more real than reality itself, they're closer to the self.
— Gao Xingjian

My interest in dreams accidentally began during my last semester in college. It's nearly 4 am, and I'm still reviewing notes for 3 final exams later that day. I had to pass because I had a job lined up the day after graduation. In dire need of sleep, I read through my list of formulas and notes one last time and crashed. What followed was a dream that had me solving engineering problems. The dream went on for what seemed like forever, solving one problem after another. When I woke up a couple of hours later, I was ready for my exams. I passed all three courses.

It was only after I returned home that I realized something special had just occurred in my sleep. My dreams had helped me pass my exams. I thought that was cool. Upon starting my new job, I quickly forgot about this capability. It took a long time before I realized how cool it was to get work answers and solutions in my dreams.

The Dreams Continue

My background is quite diverse but started traditionally. I worked as a civil servant for the US Government as a communications engineer. I designed communications facilities all over the Pacific Rim, from Adak, Alaska to Antarctica. I was also a nuclear weapons engineer for the re-entry bodies (warheads) on the Polaris, Poseidon, and Trident submarines. As an engineer, I'm very practical; I keep what works and throw out what doesn't! During my years as an engineer, author, trade book publisher, speakers bureau co-owner, professional speaker, and ordained priest, I found that dreams work! Over the past 40 years, I have taught people to use their dreams for business and personal improvement.

Solving Engineering Problems

When I began working as a communications engineer, I realized that engineering was nothing more than a series of problems that needed a solution. During my 20+ years working for the US Government, there were always problems that needed a solution. My first natural response was to complain about additional problems or the changes that were being heaped upon me. Each solution usually resulted in a series of additional changes and problems requiring more solutions. My initial reaction may have been like yours. I resented problems. Occasionally, I would get an immediate solution to a problem, but I thought it was just a lucky solution that flashed into my mind.

Fortunately, in the early 1970s, I saw an ad for a dream analysis class. I saw that the class was not being taught by a "woo-woo" instructor, but by a US Navy Commander. I immediately registered for the class because he was probably a no-nonsense military guy. I was sure that his approach was more likely to be legitimate.

The class was mind-opening. He explained how dreams helped people succeed. He then discussed what he knew from studying the writings of Carl Jung and Edgar Cayce. He talked about the use of Jung's archetypal symbols and a couple of successes he had with them.

I jumped in with my whole mind and body and delved deep into dream analysis. I read all the books I could find, which weren't very many. I even took a dream class with the Edgar Cayce Foundation and quickly realized that what they were teaching was not good enough. The ability to recognize the different types of dreams was not clear. They were vague about the meaning of different symbols. I needed to find a better solution.

Developing a Method

I got together with three educators with PhDs in sociology, education, and special education. My purpose was to discover the meaning of individual and groups of symbols. I then developed an effective method for identifying the four different types of dreams people could have and the meaning of different symbols. (I've added in a fifth type of dream.) I then put it all together and began testing it on myself and my friends. Having a lot of success in the early 1970s, I began interpreting the dreams of people I met. After a few months of successfully interpreting dreams, I began teaching a class on dream analysis and interpreted the dreams of attendees. Eventually, I began giving speeches and presenting at seminars on dream analysis.

I've done the hard work. You just have to implement the method and use the dreams you receive. If you don't understand the message, ask for another dream. If the dream is about an incident in your life and not about your question, just ask for another dream.

Lifesaving Dream

After a trip to Hawaii to see my parents, I stopped in San Francisco to see my sister, Ethel. The next morning, I woke up with the worst pain in my life in my lower belly. I practically crawled to the car and had my sister drive me to the San Francisco General Hospital. When the doctor finally came to see me, he asked me to compare my pain to the worst pain I ever had. I said I once had pleurisy and if that was a 10, this was an 11. He wouldn't allow any painkillers because it would mask my symptoms and ordered a bunch of tests. I was in the hospital, being tested and probed, doing my best to tolerate the pain.

After a battery of tests and finding nothing, the doctor said he wanted to perform exploratory surgery the next day. He told me to sign the paperwork that someone would bring in, and he left. My fading energy overcame the pain, and I slowly drifted off to sleep. In the silence of sleep, I heard a clear voice saying,

"If they cut into you, you'll die."

My body jolted as my eyes flipped wide open. Fully awake in an instant, I jerked my head from side to side, searching the room. It was eerily silent in my empty room. After a few minutes, my eyes became heavy, and I again dozed off. Again, I heard the same voice with the same message. Quickly glancing around the room, I confirmed I was still alone. I realized those scary words may have been a dream warning for me.

Having years of alternative health and healing training, I immediately began working on myself. I used what Hawayo Takata had taught me about Reiki. I also used the focusing of energy that I learned in a demonstration with Aikido founder, Morihei Ueshiba. I used pressure point massage as taught by Shiatsu. After struggling to work on my feet reflex points, I worked on the corresponding points on my hands. I used Dr. Bill Southwood's medicine cabinet method, along with Dr. Bill Dutcher's Kahuna projections. I focused it all on my painful lower stomach.

Early the next morning, I awoke pain-free. The morning blood tests and the physical exam revealed that my vital signs had returned to near normal. When the doctor came in, he was a little upset that I didn't sign the release. My condition amazed him, even as he tried to hide it. When he released me, his parting statement was,

"When you get back to Tucson and feeling a little better, consider having your appendix removed."

I verbally agreed to do that, but mentally said a double positive, "yeah, right". There was no way I was going to have an operation to remove my appendix, just for the heck of it.

When I've shared this story with people, a few rolled their eyes and gave me that same double-positive look. They usually offered a lot of theories and explanations, anything but the possibility that I had healed myself. It'd be years later, during a hernia operation, that my surgeon would find a sack where the old pain had been. He commented on how it was a very large and very old sack that had once contained something. It was the confirmation I needed—I had worked on a real physical problem and had healed myself. I believe that those 7 words I heard as I fell asleep were a dream message that saved my life.

Writing a Book

By 1980, I had many requests from people to analyze their dreams. I thought it would be best if people could analyze their dreams instead of receiving them from me. The best way to accomplish that would be to have a book they could use to analyze their dreams. So I wrote my book. I used the combined group energy of a few psychics to create my unique dictionary.

Writing a book was difficult. My communication engineering job in Hawaii was taking me all over the world. I was constantly flying to countries along the Pacific Rim. In the nuclear weapons job, I was flying to weapons facilities and Washington, DC. It was only after moving to Arizona that I finally had sufficient time to finish my book.

A Lifetime with Dreams

For several years, I gave a bi-monthly presentation at the exclusive Canyon Ranch Spa in Tucson, Arizona. I found many of the attendees were already paying attention to their dreams. Many had gained powerful insights and ideas from their dreams. Some authors shared how they used their dreams to help them create their books. The business owners and executives who were there had received dream ideas, problem solutions, and insights for their businesses. Some shared how they recalled their dreams later, as they drove to work or were having breakfast. They were in my presentation to learn how they could further use their dreams to improve the results they've been getting. A few were hoping for a personal interpretation of a specific dream.

Over many decades of researching and analyzing people's dreams, I know how dreams are so much more than people realize. Dreams have been used to gain business insights and even create new businesses; you can do the same.

With today's more complex and rapidly changing environment, creating and using an active dreaming process can be a useful tool. It has helped me while I was an engineer and as a business owner.

What's In It for You?

In your life, what would it be worth to have the insights and information you want when you need them? I feel it's priceless! Imagine being able to find solutions to problems or gain insights into situations and individuals. How valuable would it be to have a personal guide showing you the choices you have and guiding you to make the best decisions for you?

I've researched and found examples of how people have used their dreams for money and fame. I've included examples of people who've had business solutions, inventions, scientific and prophetic dreams. You'll discover a great number of successful authors and artists who've credited their dreams for their success. We'll also discuss what you can do to get the results you desire and "cashed-in." You'll understand how your dreams can serve as a powerful support tool in so many aspects of your life.

This book is a companion of my first dream book, Creative Dream Analysis: A Guide to Personal Development. That book took your random dreams and showed you how to analyze each dream. It also touched on how to program your dreams to get the message or results you wished. This book will show you examples to help you program your dreams to unleash your true, creative potential. You can then use your newfound knowledge to regain control of your dreams and your life.

What's Your Dream?

You have at least one personal aspiration or waking dream inside of you. You may be ambitious and have many more. What is it? For the ambitious ones, what are they? Are you making progress in achieving your waking dreams?

From my experience, I've found that most people have similar aspirations in their lives. They want to improve their:

- Control of Life: to shape their future, to create the life they want.

- Finance: to raise their standard of living, to afford the things they only dreamed of having.

- Career or Work: to gain the knowledge, ability, and insights to do what's required to achieve their desires.

It's also been my experience that, if you're willing, your dreams can help you achieve some or all of the above. It all begins with a strategy. The core strategy is to identify what holds you back and then remove those blocks. This is also where your dreams can help you.

In this book, you must be ready to take an active role in creating the nighttime dreams you desire. You don't have to wait for an inspiration to hit you to take action. Instead, you'll program your dreams to provide you with the answers or inspiration you need to get started. Then, your dreams will follow along in your efforts to achieve your desired results. They may continually provide you with additional insights and solutions. **As long as you specify what you wish to achieve and/or create; your dreams will do the heavy lifting to guide you there.**

Here's an example of a person who has been told in repeated dreams to organize her home office. She had made little progress when she had this dream.

> *I had a dream where I was facing a man who had a rifle. He was an expert and never missed. He aimed at me and shot his rifle. I was able to dodge the bullet as Neo did in the movie The Matrix. He was about to*

shoot another woman, and I ran up to her. Again, I was able to let the bullet miss both of us. What does this mean?

Knowing her need to clean her environment, I said the man was trying to kill the old you. But you were an expert on not taking action. You were dodging the bullet and only fooling yourself.

Oh, and I know who the shooter was. It was George Clooney, the actor.

I smiled and told her she was a professional at acting as if she was going to take action to change her life. It's time to get real and take proper action. Stop acting as if you want to do it.

Yes, we can fool other people and even try to fool ourselves. But our dreams know the truth. They know what you've said and promised, and if you were sincere or not. It knows the truth, regardless of what you may say or promise.

You Can Do It

Will my methods of using dreams for creativity and innovation always work? I believe they will. If you don't remember a dream or don't understand the message, simply ask again. Keep on trying because they've worked for so many in the past. But then, your dream life doesn't come with any guarantees. Your best bet would be to program your dreams, as you'll find later in this book. Then, as you remember and record your dreams; see the message or experiences your dreams have relayed to you. I hope they bring you much success, even more than they have given to me.

Chapter 3
Five Types of Dreams

To accomplish great things, we must not only act, but also dream; not only plan, but also believe.
— Anatole France

Let's start by understanding the process of sleep. When you fall asleep, you enter an alternating cycle of dreaming and deep sleep. Science believes that you'll experience about an hour-and-a-half of deep sleep followed by 30 minutes of dreams. If you sleep a normal 8-hour night, you'll likely have 4 of these "dream and deep sleep" cycles. The dream you remember when waking will usually be the last dream of the night.

Of course, there's nothing written in stone that says that you will follow this sequence. Edison had his dreams almost immediately after falling asleep, as you'll read later in this book. He could recall a dream after a cat nap of only a few minutes.

Then some people don't remember any of their dreams. A few may claim they only remember a few fleeting images. After a few seconds, even these quickly faded away. There're many reasons some people have problems remembering. Here are the most common:

- Waking with an alarm clock or alarm radio.
- Disturbance in the morning from children, pets, a bedmate, etc.
- Immediately getting out of bed after waking and rushing through the morning routine.
- Taking sleeping pills.
- Using recreational drugs.

On the other end of the spectrum, some recall having multiple dreams when they get up every morning. I've met dreamers who can recall minute details of all the people they met and the events that occurred in their dreams. A few of them are authors who use their dreams to write their novels. If being an author interests you, you'll find the examples in the next chapter very interesting. Here are some suggestions which will help you remember your dreams:

- Get sufficient sleep. Go to bed at a reasonable hour.
- Getting up in the middle of the night and when recalling a dream; recording it.
- Eat a heavy meal. Some say it works, but it may just be an old wives' tale.
- Have a desire to recall your dreams and be ready to record what you remember.

Types of Dreams

There are 5 basic types of dreams:

- Clearance
- Psychic Dreams
- Lucid Dreams
- Guidance Dreams
- Shared Dreams

The following quickly explains each type of dream.

Clearance Dreams

You'll experience this type of dream almost every night after falling asleep. I call them clearance dreams because they work to "clear" the stress you've accumulated during the day. They'll reproduce the problem or situation and then create a simple and quick solution. When your dreams have "solved" your first level of problems, you are ready to enter a deep level of sleep.

The dream is showing you how to release yesterday's stress or problem. But can you see how it could also tell you how to prevent that same stressor from bothering you in the future? When you receive this message, you need to implement it into your life.

Psychic Dreams

Have you ever had a psychic dream? Everyone has this type of dream regularly. Unfortunately, you probably won't remember you had a psychic dream until you have a déjà vu experience. Then, it can be a little unnerving to enter a new place and discover you're already been there. How does this happen? I believe your consciousness pierces the time/space barrier and enters a different time and space.

Purpose of Psychic Dream

Your psychic dream usually tries to prepare you for a highly probable future event. It can also show you an event from your distant past that has some relationship with your present life. The past may be of interest, but you're probably more interested in your dreams that predict a future event or situation.

Example of a Psychic Dream

You've probably heard of stories where one or both parents had dreams that their sons or daughters were seriously hurt or killed. These dreams often occur at the same moment as the actual event. I believe that parents, spouses, and friends pick up the powerful emotion generated by the person in trouble. Your psychic dreams prepare you for a future traumatic event or something happening right now. But psychic dreams can also depict any exciting or scary event in your future.

I experienced one of those intuitive flashes as I walked out of the supermarket with my wife. Suddenly, I felt the powerful need to go back in and buy a lottery ticket. Since I normally didn't buy lottery tickets, I felt that this could be a flash from an earlier dream. My wife said that if I had a feeling, I should do it. The clerk laughed when I asked for a "winning lottery ticket." The jackpot that night was worth over $8 million. We sat back and excitedly watched as we had the first 5 of 6 numbers on our ticket. Unfortunately, we didn't get the last number. But we received over a thousand dollars along with 86 other 5-number winners.

Lucid Dreams

We are not only less reasonable and less decent in our dreams... we are also more intelligent, wiser, and capable of better judgment when we are asleep than when we are awake. — Erich Fromm

In a lucid dream, you could have a most exciting and exhilarating experience. You're asleep and dreaming when you realize you're actually in a dream. It's like waking up in the morning except you're in your dream. You'll find yourself in a very exciting and empowering state. It can also be scary.

As soon as you realize you're awake in a dream, you're free to do anything you wish. As you saw in the movie The Matrix, you can be anywhere and do anything you desire. If you wish to fly, you can do that. If you want to visit the moon, that's also possible. This can be the ultimate experience, an exciting and mind-opening moment in your life. You may wonder if your life and your dreams are mirror reflections of a similar reality. After all, your experiences seem as real as they would be in your 3rd dimensional reality with one difference. You're no longer limited by the confines of a physical body and what you believe you could and couldn't do.

Ancient Masters

Of course, lucid dreaming isn't a new practice. The ancient monks and spiritual masters have used their time in their lucid dreams to make improvements in the world. But this isn't the goal I wish for you to pursue unless you want to. My goal is to make you aware of what's possible and reassure you it's a mind-opening moment of possibilities when you find yourself awake and well inside of a dream.

Guidance Dreams

These are the dreams that are the most useful for this book. You can use this type of dream to guide you on choices, provide insights, and create the ideas and solutions you desire.

Hundreds of choices are available to you every day. Right now, as you read this book, you have a dozen choices you can make. Your decision will determine whether you improve your life or make it worse.

You could continue reading this book or get up and have a snack. You could turn on the television to watch your favorite show or listen to some music. You could call a family member or visit the bathroom. Each decision from moment to moment will determine your future.

But which choice will be profitable? Which choice is the right one right now? What should I choose to do that will lead me to become famous? Who or what is an impartial advisor that can give me an idea of which one to choose? Fortunately, the source of your dreams knows you well enough to give you impartial guidance. It will provide you with suggestions, helping to make better decisions at every step of your life.

Do not waste your dreams on simple questions and minor problems. However, you may want some straight advice on the significant choices and the life-altering possibilities that face you.

Examples of Questions and Choices:

- Should I try to find a better job or remain at this one?
- Is my choice of career a good one, or should I find a different career?
- Am I being replaced by artificial intelligence or a younger person?
- Should I stay in this relationship or end it?
- Should we have children or should we put it off for a few years?
- Is this person addicted to drugs?
- Is this person telling me the truth about this investment?
- Should I continue renting or look at purchasing a house?

Many of these are tough questions. What would you be willing to pay to gain some wise insights and guidance? Well, your dreams can provide that support. After all, your dreams know you well, probably even a lot better than you know yourself.

An example is a young man who just received his MBA. He returned home to San Francisco and received 2 job offers. One was from a new social media company he had never heard of, and the other was from an Internet insurance company. He chose the insurance company and turned down the offer from Facebook. Yep, are you wondering what his career and life would have been like if he had chosen Facebook? Would he have enjoyed his job more, profited more, or been miserable? He'll never know. Now consider what it'd be worth to have your dreams guide that kind of decision? Of course, his dreams may have advised him to choose the insurance company.

Having a personal dream guide is wonderful except for one simple hitch. Your dreams use symbols to convey their message. Symbols are a great language because they are universal. They are the language of dreams.

I did not include a dictionary in this book for two reasons. First, I have a dream dictionary in my other book, Creative Dream Analysis. The second reason is you probably won't need a symbols dictionary to see the message of the dream. If you don't, you can ask for an interpretation through another dream.

Shared Dreams

I wasn't aware of this type of dream until a young lady shared it in one of my speaking presentations. She lived in California and had a dream of being with her mother, who lived on the East Coast of the United States. The dream found them together on the beach near her mother's home, and they were having a great time. They walked along the beach and talked about their lives. There seemed to be nothing unusual about this dream until she called her mother the next morning.

On the same night, her mother also had a dream about being with her daughter. They compared notes and found they both had the same dream. They even agreed on what the weather and waves were like and even described what the other was wearing. They were so excited and were looking forward to having that same type of dream again.

Naturally, it intrigued me. I had read that the aboriginal people of Australia used this method as a means of communication between family members over long distances. But it was exciting to learn that a person, half a world away from Australia, had a similar experience.

I considered this to be a special form of dreaming. It wasn't a lucid dream because neither one of them was aware they were dreaming. Instead, they simply had a normal dream, except they were both together and having the same dream.

Since then, I've had more people share their mutual dream experiences with others. Usually, it's women who share these dreams with me. Perhaps it's not that men are less caring of other people, but that women are more sensitive and more aware of the lives of friends and family members.

Here's another possible shared dream that was told to me. She was in her early 40s and shared a very interesting story. She started with,

> *"Is it possible for people to have a dream of being with another person in their future?"*

> *"Of course it's possible!" I replied. "With dreams, anything is possible."*

> *Then let me tell you what happened. I was vacationing on the Big Island of Hawaii. It was cool up in the mountains, and I went for a walk through an area with ferns and tall trees. As I walked, I felt the cool breeze, and it got a little misty. Suddenly, with no warning, a man was standing in front of me. I would usually react out of fear and turn around, but this felt different. I slowly walked up to him and we just stared at each other for a long time. We said nothing to each other as he held my gaze. It seemed so natural for me to lie back on the ground and we made love. It was wonderful, and I fell asleep. When I woke up, he was gone.*

> *A couple of months later, I'm in Honolulu and attending a meeting. When I walked in, there he was, standing on the other side of the room. He looked exactly as I remembered. I kept looking down and managed a few quick glances up at him. I couldn't look him in the eye because I was afraid he'd recognize me. As we got to know each other better, I asked him if he was on the Big Island a few months ago. He said he had not been there in a few years. So, was this something that happened, or was it just another dream?*

She had an expectant look on her face. This was not something I'd run into before. I thought for a moment, searching for an answer. There was none. So I confidently said,

> *Of course, it could have happened. But from your description, it sounds like a shared dream. If it wasn't a shared dream, then it was a third-dimensionally genuine experience or a far-out psychic experience. It doesn't matter. You simply had a wonderful experience, and that's great.*

These reports further supported my belief that our consciousness leaves our body when we fall asleep. Hence, we describe going to sleep as "falling asleep." Why do we say "falling?" And where are we falling to? We're not falling off the bed. We also say, "I drifted off," not thinking about what aspect of ourselves drifted off. Add to that the question, where do we go when we drift off?

> *I think we dream so we don't have to be apart for so long. If we're in each other's dreams, we can play together all night. — Bill Watterson*

The most commonly remembered shared dreams are most likely sex dreams. People remember these dreams because they were powerful, wonderful experiences, and exciting emotional events.

The Power of Your Dreams

Lynne Twist in The Soul of Money: Reclaiming the Wealth of Our Inner Resources stated how the culture of the Achuar people in Ecuador centered on their dreams. They consider both their dreams and their visions to be significant, and it serves as their medium of communication. They discuss their dreams and extract meaning from them. Whenever they face any important decisions, they consult their dreams.

The dreams of the Achuar showed them that there would be an eventual contact with the outside world. It also revealed that the contact would be dangerous and advised them to start the initial contact. That way, they could learn more about the outside world and handle the changes intelligently; which is what they did!

The Achuar further believes that when people change their dreams, they can change their future. They believed that, when more people understood this and created better dreams, those people could transform the world in a generation.

Remember, "It's no accident that we call our highest aspirations, dreams!"

Change Your Dreams, Change Your World

Can we begin by changing how we dream about ourselves? Is it possible to expand our dreams to include the wider area of our relationships, family, community, and country? With enough people dreaming larger and more beautiful dreams, it's possible to change the world. It all begins by saying,

"The universe is unlimited! Are our dreams large enough? What's the best dream we would like to see in our future? The universe is open to accepting our dreams!"

Perhaps the Achuar are correct and the world results from all of our dreams. In that case, we need to stop acting like savages and use our dreams wisely. The world is truly a wonderful and beautiful place. How can we best use our dreams for the good of all? This is your opportunity to discover what's possible through your dreams and make it your reality.

Chapter 4
Success Dreams for Authors

You see things; and you say, "Why?" But I dream things that never were; and I say, "Why not?"
— George Bernard Shaw

Y ou may have heard a few examples of people who have profited famously from their dreams. Some have gained great recognition and fame. Others received great wealth. Then some had their lives saved by paying attention to their dreams. Let's see if you get any insights into how you can benefit if you wished to become an author.

Author Examples

Have you ever wanted to write a book? History is filled with examples of authors who have used their dreams to write their novels or improve their non-fiction writing. The following are some well-known examples:

- **Stephen King:** While recovering from an accident, he began having vivid dreams. His dreams helped him create his novel, *Dreamcatcher*. King also credits several of his other book ideas on dreams and nightmares.

- **Stephenie Meyer:** Meyer's dreams about vampires showed her the physical make-up and character of vampires. She wove those unique ideas into her book, *Twilight*. Her series of the books have sold over 100 million copies and Hollywood has made movies of her books.

- **Mary Shelley:** (Mary Wollstonecraft Godwin, until she married Percy Bysshe Shelley) Shelley and her friends challenged each other to write scary stories to help pass the time. Thinking about the possibility of "re-animated" a corpse, she had what she called a waking dream. It was the basis for her book and the world's first science fiction novel, *Frankenstein*.

- **Robert Lewis Stevenson:** Stevenson dreamed the storyline of s book, *The Strange Case of Dr. Jekyll and Mr. Hyde*. With the aid of his dreams, he finished the first draft in three days. Nightmares are fodder for novelists specializing in horror-fantasy books.

- **Joseph Heller:** Heller got the opening lines to *Catch 22*, while he was lying in bed. Once he had the opening lines, the rest of the book quickly grew in his mind. He was so excited; he jumped out of bed and paced the floor. At work, he wrote the first chapter in longhand. An opening line was all Heller needed to fall in love with his main character.

- **Amy Tam:** Tam easily flew in her dreams with "21-cents wings." When she thought of falling, she fell. She then realized that before she was frightened, she could fly easily. When she awoke, she realized that her lack of confidence was the difference in her ability to fly. She connected that dream to the idea that she was the one holding her back. She later wrote *The Joy Luck Club*.

- **Edgar Allan Poe:** He suffered nightmares throughout his life, which inspired his poems and short stories. In *An Opinion on Dreams*, he wrote how dreams are a powerful form of consciousness.

- **Julia Slavin:** Salvin had difficulty sleeping during the 2002 sniper attacks in the Washington, DC area. Her dreams gave her the gist of her book, *Carnivore Diet*, a frightening tale that mixed a deadly and terrorizing killing spree with humor.

- **H. P. Lovecraft:** As the author of horror fiction, he got his inspiration from the vivid nightmares he suffered almost every night. The author of *The Call of Cthulhu*, he's considered one of the most significant authors of horror novels in the 20th century.

- **Richard Bach:** Bach was flying a plane when he heard a voice giving him the title of his book. After working on his book for eight years, his dream showed him the rest of his book. *Jonathan Livingston Seagull* became one of the bestselling books in history.

- **Bram Stoker:** He was interested in and had researched folklore and stories about vampires. One night, he had a dream of a vampire rising from the grave. He used that dream and the name of a historic figure, Vlad III Dracula, to write his novel, *Dracula*.

- **William Styron:** Styron has said that his novel, *Sophie's Choice*, resulted from a dream. He called it a "lingering vision" of a beautiful young woman. Her beauty mesmerized him, and it compelled him to write a book. Just having the dream image gave him different key aspects of the story. He said, "… the whole concept of the book was, if not the product of a dream itself, the product of some resonance that a dream had given me." Styron's vision of the woman was not just the impetus that compelled him to write the book, but to complete it.

- **E. B. White:** As a child, he dreamed of a tiny boy who acted like a mouse. He later began writing notes and then short stories about Stuart. Years later, he compiled it into his book, *Stuart Little*.

- **Jason Mott:** Mott's dream found him sitting at the kitchen table with his late mother. She was interested in catching up on Mott's life. The dream was so vivid he truly expected her to be sitting at the table when he walked into the kitchen the next morning. His book, *The Returned*, depicted individuals returning from the dead as they were just before they died.

- **Carlos Castaneda:** In his book, *The Art of Dreaming*, he discusses the practical possibilities and application of lucid dreaming. He describes the "4 Gates of Dreaming" and how to use lucid dreaming to travel into another person's dream.

- **Hergé:** A Belgian comic artist had nightmares of being chased by a white skeleton in a white landscape. He was told by advisors to stop and rest, but he instead created a story set in a white environment. *Tintin in Tibet* was one of his masterpieces.

- **Charlotte Bronte:** Bronte used her life experiences along with very detailed dreams as she moved in and out of consciousness to create *Jane Eyre*.

- **Dan Chaon:** He wrote The Bees after one of his son's night terror sessions of screaming and running around. When he fell back asleep, his nightmares gave him the beginning of the story.
- Gary K. Yamamoto: He wrote two children's books, three audio programs, and a business performance book with the help of his dreams.

You probably noticed that the books on the above list were mostly scary. Yes, you, along with most people, will remember scary dreams more readily than other dreams. The next time you have a nightmare, record the details and see if it could be the basis of a book. It's interesting how most of the authors above had their dreams by chance. Following the guidance found later in this book, you can choose to create your book in whatever genre you wish. With the help of your dreams, you have no limits.

I started my publishing business to publish my first dream book. When my partner asked if I could write a children's book, I agreed. I wrote my first children's book, *Jason's Journey into the Rainbow*, from two nights of dreams. I wrote my second children's book, *Jason in the Land of the Dragons*, from one night's dream. Of course, the books required editing, an artist to do the illustrating, and an illustrated cover.

My three children's audio programs were each created from a single night of dreaming. I then needed to have the music and a song to go with the story. I programmed my dreams and woke up with a song, both the words and the melody. Not being a professional musician, I didn't know how to capture both the words and tune. My wife came to my rescue and made me sing the song into a recorder. As reluctant as I was, I sang the songs and had a professional musician create the music. My wife and two friends sang and created the music for the program. I donated two of the audio versions to a religious, educational program.

For my performance book, *Professional Power, Personal Excellence*, my dreams made me realize that a person's performance depended on two factors, their ability and their behavior. My book shows people how to improve these critical factors to excel in their professional careers and personal lives.

As a regular speaker on dreams at the famous Canyon Ranch in Tucson, Arizona, there were many authors in the audience. After my dream presentation, I spoke with individuals in the audience. I discovered how different novelists used their dreams to gain insight into the lives of the characters in their books. They learned how people dressed, how they spoke, what they ate, and even what their thought processes were. With this background, they could add significant details to the characters. If you're an author or an aspiring author, consider using your dreams to enhance your writing.

You as an Author

Here's how to use the experiences of the authors to create or improve our present or future books:

- **Record the storyline:** Capture the idea of what's happening in your dream. When you look at what's written, it may not be enough for a book. Ask for the rest of the story and be ready to record your dream.

- **See what is different or unique:** Stephenie Meyer was aware enough in her dreams that she could see vampires in another light. That allowed her to capture unique details about their nature and translate them into her wonderful books and movie.

- **Having a nightmare:** Nightmares can provide a unique book. It could be pure horror, science fiction, or something unique. It's time to go beyond alien encounters and the living dead. The scarier the nightmare, the better the novel or movie script.

- **Short stories:** Joseph Heller thought he had only enough material to write a novella. Fortunately, additional dreams allowed it to grow into a full novel. E. B. White did the same with his short stories and then compiled them to create Stuart Little.

- **Scary event:** The COVID-19 Pandemic has probably created enough nightmares to create thousands of books. Each one is probably different, set in an unfamiliar environment, absolutely scaring the reader or moviegoer. People love horror novels and short stories. Why? Could it be because their lives are boring? So if you have an over-the-top nightmare, it may excite you enough to write a novel.

- **Be patient:** Richard Bach had to wait years to finish his book. The successful authors I met at Canyon Ranch Spa described their dreams give them material so they could add color and authenticity to their novels.

- **A unique point of view:** Perhaps your dream gives you a different perspective. Jason Mott had a dream so real he believed his late mother actually visited him. It was enough of a storyline that allowed him to write a book on people returning from death and acting as if they have never died.

Your dreams are unlimited. Remember, your dreams not only help you by keeping you safe and solving problems, but they can also help in your creativity. Don't sleep through another night and miss a potential bestseller.

Becoming an Author

Not that long ago, becoming an author was such a tedious task. I know, because I founded and ran a trade book publishing company back in the 1980s. I did this because it was extremely difficult to get my dream book published. Fortunately, the process of self-publishing is so much easier today. If you wish to share your story, knowledge, or nightmare, you simply have to type it on a computer or handwrite it on a paper tablet. There are inexpensive ways to get your book written, edited, typeset, published, and available for sale on Amazon. If you have any problems along the way, your dreams can help you get over any mental roadblocks. When it comes time to market your book, your dreams can also offer suggestions.

Why should you wish to become an author? As an author, people interested in your topic see you as an authority. You can see it in the word "authority." The first six letters of the word authority are "author."

Chapter 5
Success Dreams for Lottery Winners

The poor man is not he who is without a cent, but he who is without a dream.

— Harry Kemp

The following are lottery winners who willingly reveal to the world they hit a small, large, and mega jackpot with the help of their dreams. I can understand why most people remained anonymous whenever they could. So, take a moment and imagine what your life could become if you were the next winner of the lottery because of a dream. Here are some of their stories:

Instant Winners

- **Kevin Miller:** Kevin dreamed about winning a lottery prize. A few days later, he was on his way to work when he stopped at a Circle K to buy a lottery ticket. He stood in line behind a guy who was taking such a long time. At one point, he almost gave up. But he waited and his patience paid off; he bought his ticket and won $250,000.

- **Deana Sampson:** Deana had a dream of her deceased brother who told her she would win the jackpot. Life was hard for her, with several deaths of close family members, including her brother. She won £5,400,000 the next day.

- **Philip Poultney:** Philip had a vivid dream of winning the lottery. His dream showed him purchasing the ticket from the supermarket he visited, checking the ticket there, and being told to call Camelot because it was a big prize. The next day, he had his ticket checked at the supermarket and recognized the sound of the winning ticket. He thought he had won £20,000, but it turned to be £1,000,000.

- **The Smith Family:** This family won the $429 million Powerball Jackpot in October 2013. One member of the family dreamed his relatives were saying the lucky numbers. The next day she bought 10 Mega Million tickets. Knowing the numbers were lucky, she used them in different combinations, along with his birth month, date, and year.

- **Kaila Moore:** Kaila dreamed she had bought a scratch-off on August 29, 2020. Even though she had never bought a lottery ticket before, she did so the next day. She won $100,000 and took home $70,756 after taxes.

- **Mary Wollens:** A few days before the lottery drawing, Mary dreamed of all six numbers for the $24 million lottery drawing on 9/30/2006. She was so sure the dream was prophetic that she bought a second lottery ticket with the same numbers. She won and claimed two-thirds of the jackpot because she had two winning tickets. Her share totaled $16 million.

- **Victor Amole:** Amole dreamed a series of numbers. He used them in the Virginia Lottery's Cash 5 game. It was for the January 13, 2018 game. He was so sure that he bought 4 tickets with the same numbers. Each ticket won $100,000 for $400,000. Amole is another committed dreamer.

- **Deborah Rose:** Rose from Ontario had a dream of six birds circling her. She didn't know what the dream meant, but used the numerology numbers from each letter of the word "B-I-R-D-S" (2, 9, 18, 4, 19) and then added the number 6 for 6 birds. She won $750,000 on the Ontario Lottery.

Sometimes Patience Is Required

- **Australian Man:** An anonymous Australian man had a dream that gave him the winning lottery numbers. After playing the lottery for 13 years, he won $1,000,000 AU. He knew that one day he would see all of his numbers on the ticket he held.

- **Australian Woman:** In her dream, she watched the numbers appear one by one. She played those numbers and continued for 15 years. It paid off when she won a $700,000 lottery jackpot.

- **Olga Beno:** Olga was a lottery enthusiast and played the lucky numbers she received in a dream. She won a few small sums, but never game up. After 30 years, her numbers came up, and she won $5,366,704 Canadian. The timing was perfect as her medical bills threatened financial ruin.

- **Deng Pravatoudom:** Deng's dream showed her winning lottery numbers. She didn't win quickly, but continued playing the numbers for 20 years. On December 1, 2020, she won a $60,000,000 LOTTO MAX jackpot from the Ontario Lottery. The numbers didn't win, but she won a Free Play and the Free Play won her the final Jackpot.

Misses or Sad Stories

- **Becca Jeffries:** Becca had a dream of riding a horse and balls with numbers were jumping at her. Her car had 2 flat tires, so she called her husband and told him to buy a ticket for that night's $64,000,000 jackpot drawing. When she saw the numbers on the drawing, they all matched her numbers. She was so excited and called her husband to tell him they had won the lottery. He said he hadn't bought a ticket because he didn't think she was serious.

- **Gary Searle:** Gary always maintained that the lottery was a waste of time. One day, his dad said he should buy a ticket because he was lucky. To prove his point, Gary wrote 6 numbers and watched the lottery drawing that evening. All 6 of the winning lottery numbers matched what he had on the paper. He could have been an instant millionaire.

- **Suzette Alispach:** She jumped out of bed with the lottery numbers, put on her shoes, and ran to the convenience store a block away. There was a long line as she kept repeating the lottery numbers. When it was finally her turn, she could only recall three numbers. Those numbers matched the drawn numbers, but she didn't win.

- **A Relative of Mine:** She had a dream that gave the winning numbers to the lottery. She began running around the house, looking for paper and a pen or pencil. She kept running and when she finally found what she needed, she could only recall three of the dream lottery numbers. The three numbers came up that evening. Ditto the above.

Biggest Jackpot

They drew the largest lottery jackpot on January 13, 2016, for $1.59 billion US. Now that's some serious money, which was split by 3 winners who each received over $500 million, US. Winning the lottery changes people's lives and the people in their lives.

Winning any lottery because of a dream is wonderful. Unfortunately, there's no way to guarantee you'll be the next lottery winner. However, I would recommend you have paper and pen next to your bed, in case you get lottery numbers. The above examples may motivate you to go out and get a lottery ticket. Others may program their dreams to get winning lottery numbers, and it may improve their chance of winning. Then there are those who say they never win and refuse to take a chance. Above all, never spend more than you can afford to lose.

You as a Lottery Winner or Player

Instant winners

- **Kevin Miller:** If you dreamed you won a lottery prize, how long would you wait in a long or slow line? It could make the difference between winning and not winning.

- **Deana Sampson:** This was a simple dream to fulfill. All she had to do was to buy a ticket. No numbers to memorize and write, no need to know which lottery, just buy a ticket. If you had a similar dream, will you go out and buy a lottery ticket.

- **Philip Poultney:** He already had his ticket. His dream only told him to check his ticket to win. I know of a couple of people who often forget to check on their lottery tickets and the ticket expired. This dream may have been a reminder not to forget to check the ticket or misplace it.

- **The Smith Family:** If you had the numbers from relatives in a dream and were missing a number, would you buy enough tickets and add what intuitively felt like the right numbers? Picking numbers is like getting a sense or a gut feeling that something is right. It paid off big for the Smith Family.

- **Mary Wollens:** She was so sure her dream was correct; she got two tickets with the same numbers. Now that was a total commitment to the dream message.

- **Victor Amole:** was so sure that he bought four tickets with the same numbers. When you have a powerful winning lottery dream, will you commit yourself to buying more than one ticket?

- **Deborah Rose:** How cool to use numerology. I understand numerology. I'm assuming she's an expert in numerology. So her dreams saw numerology as a convenient way to communicate with her.

Patience Required

- For everyone in this category, congratulations on believing in your dreams. I'm not sure if I could keep playing the same number for over 10 years. That's a total commitment to a dream. Congratulations again.

Missed or Sad Stories

- **Becca Jeffries:** All I can say is ouch! When someone asks to buy a lottery ticket, please buy it. If you're like me, you're probably wondering what happened between Becca and her husband when he got home.

- **Gary Searle:** I hope this incident corrected his beliefs about the lottery. When he randomly wrote his numbers, did you wonder where he got those from? I would like to say that it may have been from an earlier dream. I'm also wondering what his dad said to him afterward.

- **Suzette Alispach and my relative:** The simple remedy is to keep a pen and paper next to your bed. The other choice is having a small tape recorder next to your bed. Be sure you can turn it on and off in the dark.

When You Win!

Here are the steps to take when you win a large sum from the lottery:

- Sign the back of your lottery ticket.
- Don't tell anyone you won the lottery. Try to maintain your anonymity when collecting your winnings. You can become a target for kidnappers, scammers, and people who want your help.
- Know how long you have before you have to present your winning ticket. There is an expiration date.
- Change your phone number and address, in case word of your winning gets out.
- Find a lottery lawyer to help set up your finances.
- Get a financial advisor team to help you invest your money.
- Have an accounting team do the number crunching. Just remember to keep all your receipts.
- Change nothing for at least 6 months. People will look for anyone who skyrockets their spending.
- Pay off all your debts. Even if you lose all the rest, you'll be debt-free.
- Deactivate your social media accounts. People quickly notice an upgrade in lifestyle.
- Don't loan money to loved ones. If they need the money, make it a gift.

Finally, stay healthy. This includes staying active, eating a healthy diet, and maintaining contact with old friends.

Chapter 6
Success Dreams for Businesses and Inventors

It's the possibility of having a dream come true that makes life interesting.
— Paulo Coelho

If you've watched the financial news channels, you realize how many new businesses are coming online. Technology was first used to replace manual labor. But today, some people imagine life on an extraordinary level. Inventions to eliminate global warming, pollution, waste, and unlimited energy are just some areas that are being reimagined. I believe that much of the source of this comes from our dreams. Here are a few examples from those who shared the power found in their dreams.

Business Examples

- **Larry Page:** He was a graduate student at Stanford majoring in computer science. He had a dream about cataloging the links to every website on the entire Internet. When he got up, he realized how quickly the Internet was expanding and wondered if it was even possible. With the help of Sergey Brin, they created Google, which then grew to become the major part of the parent company Alphabet.

- **Dennis Hong:** When Hong went to bed, he imagined different shapes floating and assembling. He got up during the night to record his dreams. In the morning, he looked to see if he found anything interesting. He recorded any useful or novel ideas on his computer. He has created practical applications for robotics, GPS, cars for the blind, etc.

- **Floyd Ragsdale:** DuPont's Kevlar machine had problems with constant downtime. Ragsdale had a dream where he saw a Kevlar machine that didn't have a problem. Looking closely, he found the machine had springs inserted inside the tubes. When he shared his dream idea with his boss, he was told to forget about it. After work, he stayed back and secretly placed springs inside the tubes. The machine worked perfectly after that.

- **Phil Martens:** He was head of Ford's new product development group in 2002. Phil woke up with a dream revelation on how to lower production costs by sharing designs between similar models.

- **Rose O'Neill:** O'Neill created the Kewpie Doll characters based on a dream. Ladies' Home Journal asked Rose to write a series on her dolls. She wrote verses so they would have their own stories.

- **Gary K. Yamamoto:** As an electrical engineer, he used his dreams to help him design the installation of several communications systems, including the complete upgrade of the Naval Communication Station, in Guam. He also dreamed and created the Standard Plans Program for the US Navy, which reduced the time and effort required to design and upgrade all communications systems and facilities. Another dream gave him the solution to prevent the unintended breakup of the Poseidon reentry body (warhead) launched from nuclear submarines.

You in a Business

In today's rapidly changing environment, your job or business requires constant improvements. Fixes and improvements seem to grow out of problems or difficult situations. When you face problems at work, you could program your dreams to provide a solution. Your dreams can also help you simplify a process, enhance service, and even create a new product. Take a moment to look at your job or career. Is there anything that an improvement or enhancement would improve sales, maintenance, or service? There's no end to what your dreams can do to help you.

Here are some insights from the above dream solutions:

- **What if:** If you had an impossible dream, would you wonder if it could come true? Larry Page had the computer programming skills to make his dream real. But today, it's the idea that's powerful. There are many people who have the skills but lack the creative idea or innovative solution.

- **Look from another point of view:** You could do what Dennis Hong does. He uses his imagination to create images. If that doesn't work for you, you could read a book or magazine on a different subject. Then, when getting up in the morning, you can imagine 6 impossible things before breakfast, as Alice did in Louis Carroll's book, Alice in Wonderland.

- **Just do it:** When your dream has provided a solution, just do it. It may work fine as it did for Floyd Ragsdale. Even if it didn't, at least you tried. It's well known that more significant innovations and unique ideas end up in the graveyard when the inventor dies.

As the co-owner of a speakers bureau, I used my engineering skills, background, and dream inspirations to create computer solutions. Back in the dark ages of computers, I automated much of our business to simplify our work.

As the CEO of an extensive business, would it be helpful to have all employees recording their dreams for creative ideas and innovative solutions? It may appear to be a risky proposition for CEOs to consider implementing unproven ideas and improvements. But all substantial businesses involved some risk.

Inventor Examples

The following are examples of people who used their dreams to enhance their creativity or discover an innovative solution to the problems they were facing. Here are a few inventor examples.

- **Thomas Edison:** Edison worked purposely to get his creative insights. His creative process was to take naps. He would sit in his chair that had an empty steel pan next to the chair. He would hold a few steel balls in his hand above the steel pan and took what we would describe as a catnap. As he fell asleep, his fingers relaxed and eventually the balls would slip out of his hand. As the balls hit the pan, the clanging would wake him. He would often get up with a new idea or a viable solution to his latest project.

- **Elias Howe:** Howe could not figure out how to make the needle on his sewing machine work. One night, he had a dream where scary-looking natives took him prisoner. When the warriors were about to execute him, he noticed the spears they were threatening him with had holes near the tip. He woke up with inspiration from his dream and drilled a hole near the tip of the needle. He then inserted the thread into the needle and his sewing machine worked perfectly.

- **D.B. Parkinson:** At Bell Labs, he was designing a carded potentiometer for telephones. One night, his dream showed Allies troops in England accurately shooting down enemy planes using his potentiometer. He immediately adapted his potentiometer to mount onto the antiaircraft gun control to control the guns automatically. They credited his invention for destroying German bombers using fewer shells and for shooting down 89 of 91 V-1 buzz bombs Germany launched against England.

- **Madam C. J. Walker:** When Walker lost her hair from a scalp infection; she tried to find a solution. After many failures, she had a dream where a man told her what to mix to create her hair treatment. Some ingredients were exotic, and she had to import them from foreign countries. The mixture worked, and she became the first American woman, a self-made millionaire.

You as an Inventor:

To be successful in this category, it would be easier if you were working in this field. Having the right background and knowledge makes it easier for you to recognize a valid solution in your dreams. For instance, it helps if you have some technical knowledge to develop a new manufacturing process. Without the right knowledge, you may get an insight into a creative idea or an innovative solution, but then can't see the genius of what you have. Even if you saw the dream's insight's potential, you may not express it properly to create a workable product or service.

- **Take short naps:** You can use your cell phone to wake you a few minutes after you take a nap. Before you close your eyes, think of the problem you want to solve. When your alarm wakes you, recall your dream. See how it can provide you with a solution. The solution may be priceless.

- **Waking with a dream:** Consider the dream in line with the solution or idea you were looking for. It may be obvious or it may take a little thought or work to discover the message of the dream.

All the people in the above examples were working on a problem. Do you have a problem you need to solve? Your dreams can help.

Chapter 7
Success Dreams for Scientists and Mathematicians

I know what you're probably thinking; all the people in this category are scientists and are smart or bordering on genius. They are working on things, which are beyond what most people can comprehend. Yet, I included them here to show you that even these people have benefited from their dreams.

- **Niels Bohr:** He's the father of quantum mechanics and the winner of the Nobel Prize for Physics. He had a dream showing him the structure of the atom where the nucleus was in the center, with electrons spinning around it, similar to the planets spinning around the sun.

- **Albert Einstein:** Einstein dreamed he was sledding down a steep mountain and was approaching the speed of light. Looking around, he saw the stars had changed their shape. He contemplated on his dream experience and it led him to formulate his general theory of relativity. There are other accounts of how other dreams gave him the basis for his special theory of relativity.

- **James Watson:** He was working on the shape and structure of DNA when he had a dream of two intertwined snakes with heads at opposite ends. Other accounts reported his dream showed him a double-sided staircase. Both dreams revealed the correct structure of the DNA.

- **Nikola Tesla:** As an engineer and inventor, Tesla used his dreams for inspiration and created the alternating current generator, remote control, induction motor, 3-phase power, neon lamp, the x-ray machine, radio communication, and many other inventions. And no, he's not currently working alongside Elon Musk at Tesla.

- **Alfred Russel Wallace:** Wallace created the theory of evolution a year before Charles Darwin published his findings. While collecting bird specimens in Indonesia, he suffered from a fever. His dream hallucinations revealed how only the fittest survived in the animal kingdom. He was the founder of the theory of evolution by natural selection.

- **Friedrich August Kekulé:** He dreamed of how larger atoms united with smaller ones to form chains. This was the foundation of his Structural Theory of Molecules. While working on the shape of the benzene molecule, his dream showed him how atoms were forming into the shape of snakes. One snake bit his tail and appeared to be mocking him. In the morning, he realized the dream's meaning and solved the circular shape of the Benzene molecule. This breakthrough insight gave scientists a new understanding of all aromatic compounds.

- **Dmitri Mendeleyev:** Mendeleyev fell asleep while chamber music was being played in the next room. We base music on 8 primary notes. In his dream, he observed individual elements falling and arranging themselves into 8 columns. The result is the periodic table which forms the basis of chemistry.

- **Louis Agassiz:** As a naturalist, Agassiz struggled to reconstruct the fossilized imprint of a fish partially hidden in a stone slab. On different nights, he had three fish dreams. In the third dream, he drew what he saw in his dream without turning on the light. When he got up, he followed his sketch and safely removed the particles hiding the fish fossil.

The above list is a wide range of how dreams helped to advance science's efforts to understand and create the life and environment we enjoy today. While these are examples of solving immense problems, your dreams could help you solve your problems, even if they appear to be small.

You as a Scientist

In the scientific field, it's amazing that these people actually admitted that their ideas and solutions came through their dreams. Scientists are people who deal with observations and the facts they encounter. Even theoretical scientists would rarely admit to getting insights from their dreams. They would credit contemplation, a sudden insight, or a flash of inspiration. But as I mentioned before, those insights probably originated in their dreams. How much more could they have done if they programmed their dreams to give them the insights they were looking for.

- **What you're working on:** Whatever dream you get, look at it as a solution to the problem you've been working on. While it is sometimes obvious, it usually requires a bit of work to understand the true meaning of the dream.

- **Becoming ill:** two examples listed an illness as the cause of the insight or solution. There is a strong correlation because the thinking mind shuts down when a person is ill. A word of caution: do not get sick to solve a problem.

If this is your field, your dreams are always there to help and guide you. You can program your dreams and ask for ideas and solutions. While it may sound far out for you in this field, my question is; would it hurt to find out what's possible? Even if you fail, no one has to know!

Math Examples

- **Srinivasa Ramanujan:** He was one of India's greatest mathematical geniuses who proved almost 4,000 theorems in his lifetime. In his dreams, the Hindu goddess Shree Lakshmi Namagiri would present him with mathematical functions. Ramanujan would have a hunch about how they behaved. As soon as he woke up, he would write these math functions down, and then work to verify them. The movie, The Man Who Knew Infinity, is about his life and discoveries. It has taken 100 years for researchers to prove him right.

- **Henri Poincaré:** In his lifetime, he struggled to create a method to solve an entire group of equations. After contemplating the problem for a long time, he would fall asleep. When he woke up, he found the solution written on several sheets of paper next to his bed. His works covered celestial mechanics, fluid mechanics, optics, thermodynamics, quantum theory, the theory of relativity, etc.

I used my sleep to help me solve math and engineering problems for many years. However, that's nothing compared to what you may find possible if you were to specialize in math and/or science.

You as a Mathematician

The key to using your dreams is to be aware of them. You can program your dreams to solve any problem you're working on. Your dreams may carry a new idea or solution that quickly fades away unless you're alert and capture them. You must record your dreams on a recorder or paper. Then see if they hold anything you can use.

- **Deity or Angel:** If a divine being helps you solve problems; that would be wonderful. If a deity comes to you with expert knowledge, please use it.

- **Sleep writing:** Contemplating on a problem before going to sleep can give you the solution you want. Remember to keep paper and pen next to your bed.

These two dreamers are unique. They set a new level of what you can expect from your dreams.

Chapter 8
Success Dreams for Entertainers

When entertainers have dreams, I've wondered if they dream tunes which they can turn into a song or music piece. As you'll read below, my music experience is elementary school level. But for musicians, music is their language. I don't know if they regularly dream music, but I'm sure they can program themselves to that. Perhaps that's what Steve Allen did in order to compose over 8,500 songs, as you'll read below.

Entertainer Examples

- **Paul McCartney:** As a member of the Beatles, McCartney woke up with a tune in his head. He said it had come to him in his dream. He used that melody and composed the hit tune, "Yesterday". When the Beatles were about to break up, Paul had a dream about his mother, who passed away when he was 14. She reassured him and said to "let it be." He started writing that song the next day.

- **Jimi Hendrix:** He had just read a sci-fi novel and went to sleep. In his dream, he walked under the sea before a purple haze slowly surrounded him. It was the inspiration for his composition "Purple Haze."

- **John Lennon:** Another member of the Beatles wrote a bestselling song, "#9 Dream" based on a dream he had. Who knows how many other songs Lennon's dreams influenced or it created.

- **Sting:** In the middle of the night, Sting suddenly woke up. In his head was the line, "every breath I take, I'll be watching you." He got out of bed and sat at his piano. In 30 minutes, he had written the song.

- **Billy Joel:** Joel's dreams provide him with a lot of song ideas and he often struggled to remember them. "The River of Dreams" was a song that just wouldn't go away. He finally decided that it was a sign for him to work on it. It became the title track to his 1993 album.

- **Wolfgang Amadeus Mozart:** He once wrote, "Nor do I hear in my imagination the parts successively, I hear them all at once. What a delight this is! All this inventing, this producing, takes place in a pleasing, lively dream.

- **Elvis Costello:** Costello woke up with a song and searched for a guitar. Not finding one, he turned on the cassette recorder in the kitchen and began singing. He used his hand to slap the kitchen counter and recorded the song on a cassette player "Honey, Are You Straight or Are You Blind." You can hear that beat in his recording.

- **Steve Allen:** Allen composed the theme song for his show, The Steve Allen Show. The song, "This Could Be the Start of Something Big" came to him in a dream. As a prolific composer of over 8,500 songs. He claimed he composes his songs while driving, taking a shower, or at work. I have to wonder how many of his songs were first created in his dreams and remembered later.

- **Christopher Nolan:** From his lucid dreams, he created the psychological thriller movie "Inception." The plot follows a dream thief who steals dreams from CEOs and business tycoons.

- **Richard Linklater:** As a movie director, Linklater used his dreams as inspiration for some of his films. He experienced lucid dreaming and used that theme for his movie, "Waking Life".

- **Todd Rundgren:** His dream gave him the complete composition of "Bang the Drum All Day." He then rushed to the studio or began recording everything he remembered from his dream.

- **Richard D. James / Aphex Twin:** He wrote the music for his "Elected Ambient Works, Volume II" by sleeping and sometimes having lucid dreams in the studio. When he got up, he immediately wrote what he heard in his dreams.

- **Giuseppe Tartini:** Tartini had a dream where he handed the devil a violin. The devil then played the most beautiful piece he had ever heard. When he awoke, he tried to recreate the sounds of his dream.

Failing to do that, he wrote one of his greatest works, "The Devil's Trill," based on that dream experience.

- **James Cameron:** When he was 19 years old, Cameron had a dream of a bioluminescent forest and glowing trees. He woke up very excited, sketched what he saw in his dream, and then painted it. He used those images when creating his hit movie, "Avatar." He was ill on another occasion and had a dream where a robot dragged itself along the floor with a knife. It was the inspiration for the movie "Terminator".

- **Johnny Cash:** Cash had a dream where he met Queen Elizabeth. The Queen said he was like a thorn bush, caught in a whirlwind. Reading the Book of Revelations reminded him about the dream and he composed, "The Man Comes Around." In another dream, he got the idea of using mariachi horns in the song "Ring of Fire."

- **Gary K. Yamamoto:** With the help of his dreams, he created the words and music for his three children's audio program.

I know I'm repeating myself, but I wanted to point out I have no music training. Sure, I played the guitar, but I only knew how to strum some basic chords. So, with this limited knowledge of music, I could create three simple songs for my audio program.

You as an Entertainer

If you're a professional or an aspiring professional, think of what you could do when you're able to get the music and words from your dreams. Makes you wonder if any of the Oscar winners ever got their inspiration or even the entire songs from their dreams. I'll put in one example of what occurs.

- **Whenever it comes:** Music is in the life blood of a musician. As a musician, you need to be ready to record whenever the music flows. You can program yourself and expect to have a dream with a song.

- **Always ready to capture the music:** For musicians and entertainers, your dreams can be a continuous process of creativity and innovation. You need to be aware and ready to capture what you find in your dreams. A simple small digital recorder is most helpful. If your instrument is not nearby, hum it or sing it into the recorder. The important thing is to capture it as soon as possible before it fades away.

Chapter 9
Success Dreams for Medical Personnel

The medical field is wide open to innovation through dreams. Every medical professional can use their dreams to investigate so many procedures, drugs, and processes. This is a great opportunity.

Medical Examples

- **Frederick Banting and Charles Best:** Frederick Banting dreamed that the cause of diabetes was the lack of insulin. Another dream revealed to him how to develop insulin. With the help of Charles Best, Banting isolated the compound that saved and changed the lives of millions of diabetics. Banting received the Nobel Prize in Medicine.

- **Agusto Odon:** His son Lorenzo had a rare disease resulting in brain degeneration. Augusto fell asleep in the library and dreamed of a chain of paperclips and saw that his son, Lorenzo, was pulling on the chain. When he awoke, he realized the chain represented only one type of fat that was causing his son's disease and not the two that the doctors believed. He and his wife Michaela found someone to develop an oil mixture that solved the problem. It's called "Lorenzo's Oil," and their son lived 22 years longer than the doctors had predicted. Naturally, you may wonder how Agusto realized the paperclip chain represented one type of fat. He was astute enough to see the connection between the chain and the oil that was causing his son's disease.

- **Forrest Gale Wellington:** Wellington was a unique veterinarian who often took a nap to solve tough cases. His dreams provided him with solutions on how to perform the needed operation. Upon waking, he would use his hands to describe to his assistants how they would do what they previously thought to be impossible.

- **Otto Loewi:** He believed that nerve impulses were chemically rather than electrically transmitted. He couldn't prove his theory until a dream showed him how. For his work, he won the Nobel Prize for Medicine.

- **Edgar Cayce:** People referred to Cayce as the "sleeping prophet" and said we will preview every significant event in our lives by at least one dream. He used his dreams to tell people how to heal themselves, to educate people on possibilities, and to advance dream research.

- **Jonas Salk:** He discovered and developed the first successful polio vaccine. He said, "I have had dreams, and I've had nightmares. I overcame the nightmares because of my dreams.

On a personal note, I've known Dr. Forrest Gale Wellington for over 35 years. I was privileged to watch him work with both the animals and their owners. I've also had the privilege of having him work on me on so many occasions. I've met so many people who referred to him as a "miracle worker" for how he helped and healed them. Between his dreams, his knowledge, and his intuitive insights, he was a gifted doctor.

You in the Medical Field

If you're in the medical field, you can use your dreams to go beyond the known.

- **A quick nap:** when faced with a procedure that is beyond what you know, a nap could prove helpful. While Dr. Wellington made it look easy, a nap would not hurt the patient but could produce a new and effective procedure.

- **A channeled solution:** Edgar Cayce would sleep and give the solution to medical problems in patients he had not met. There are very few people who can do this. Because Cayce could do this means that others may do what he did.

But before you try any medical procedures your dreams suggest, please consult with your doctor. If you are a doctor or a medical researcher, there are many health and medical problems that could benefit from a dream insight. Program your dreams and see how they can assist you.

Chapter 10
Success Dreams in Artists

Art is a wide-open field for using your dreams for creative ideas and processes. While most of the artists shown here work in painting, there is a need for art in everything. Creative dream ideas help architects in designing their buildings, store owners in setting up their displays, and even home gardeners designing their backyard plants and lights. There is art in everything, and a dream can inspire any artist.

Art Examples

- **Salvador Dali:** The surrealist painter has called many of his works "hand-painted dream photographs." An actual dream inspired his famous work, "Persistence of Memory" depicting melting clocks. He considered dreams as central to human thought.

- **Leonardo da Vinci:** He was an astronomer, sculptor, geologist, mathematician, botanist, animal behaviorist, inventor, engineer, architect, and even a musician. On dreams he wrote, "Why does the eye see a thing more clearly in dreams than the imagination when awake?"

- **Michael Barnsley:** Barnsley had the same nightmare for over 20 years before realizing it had a purpose. It showed him how to take photos (such as maps shot from space) and automatically collages them together to provide a photo of infinite resolution. It's what we see when we look up maps on the Internet.

- **Jasper Johns:** He was struggling to become an artist. One night, he had a dream of himself painting an enormous flag. After the dream, he painted his best-known piece, "Flag," and his career took off. His works sell for millions ($110 million in 2010) and Flag is listed as the most paid for a living artist. He even paid for any of his works, previous to Flag, that came to him and destroyed them.

- **Vincent Van Gogh:** Van Gogh has stated, "I dream my painting and I paint my dream." He is basically saying much if not all of his art was depicting his dreams. If you're an artist, you can do the same, and you don't have to cut off an ear.

- **Jim Shaw:** He put together a collection of his pencil drawings that depicted the world of his dreams, revealing his fears, obsessions, and sexual fantasies. His book, Dreams, includes his works.

- **Max Magnus Norman:** Norman paints his visions and images that he sees while in a meditative state or in his dreams. It gives his art a realistic appearance, as you might see them in your dreams.

- **Elle Nicolai:** Nicolai translates images and symbols from her dreams and creates her art in 3-dimensional reality.

You as an Artist

If you're an artist or work in any artistic endeavor, consider using your dreams for ideas. Your dreams don't care what medium you work in, whether it's pencil, paint, or clay.

- **Sketch pad:** Have this next to your bed. When you have a dream with a scene you wish to capture, you can sketch it. Be prepared to do this because, like all dreams, an image may quickly fade away.

You could use your dreams to help you design a marketing piece or how to better layout an ad or create a brochure. If you're a self-published author, your dreams could depict or improve your book cover. As a photographer, you could use your dreams to help you stage your subjects and background for the next day's shoot. Your dreams can guide you in any field you wish. You simply have to call on them and listen to their advice. The simple yet effective method to do this is coming later in this book.

Chapter 11
Success Dreams for Psychics

Have you ever wondered what the future holds for you? You have a wonderful way to find out. As Edgar Cayce, the great sleeping prophet, has said, "every significant event in your life will be previewed by at least one dream." If you're thinking it's impossible, have you ever had a déjà vu moment in your life? Your dreams allowed you to visit that moment to prepare you for the experience. Here are a few of the most well-known cases.

Prophetic Examples

- **Abraham Lincoln:** Lincoln had a dream two weeks before his assassination. In it, he heard people crying, and a soldier told him the president had been shot and killed. Looking at the body, he realized it was him. Before the assassination, Lincoln told General Grant that his dreams foretold an event of national significance. It's recorded that General Grant tried to stop the President from going to Ford's theater, but the President went anyway.

- **Isaac Frauenthal:** He dreamed that the Titanic would crash into something and sink. The dream kept repeating itself when he was on board the Titanic. Being alerted to the danger, he survived the sinking, along with his brother and his brother's wife. This is just another of over 150 verified accounts of Titanic-related prophecies.

- **Eryl Mai Jones:** She was just 10 years old when she told her mother she was "not afraid to die" and she will be with her friends, Peter and June. One day she said, "I dreamed I went to school and there was no school there. Something black had come down all over it!" The next day, the mountain of coal waste broke loose and covered her school, killing Eryl, her two friends, and many others.

- **Lynyrd Skynyrd:** Jo Jo Billingsley was to rejoin the Lynyrd Skynyrd band in two days. That night, she had the most vivid dream that the plane crashed. The next day, she called to warn them not to get on the plane. The band members voted and said this would be the last time they flew on that plane. Her dream became a reality the next day when they flew in a raging snowstorm and the plane crashed.

- **Jerry Rice:** He was an NFL wide receiver. On the night before a game, he would have dreams of him playing football. The next day, playing in an NFL game, the dreams he had would come true.

- **Charlotte Marie Stevens:** Her grandmother had a dream for 3 nights. Each dream showed a woman standing at the end of her bed, telling her to move her mother and aunt out of their bedroom. Charlotte's mother and aunt moved into another bedroom. On the third night, the roof collapsed and a massive beam fell across their former beds. When her grandmother described the woman to her father, he said the messenger was his mother who had died when he was young.

Edgar Cayce said that everyone will preview every significant event in their lives with at least one dream. Your dreams will do this to prepare you for your future. Your dream may show you a future relationship or even a new job you should consider. Or it could give you an insight on where to go on a trip and what to avoid. Remember, your dreams have only one client, you! It has only one purpose: to help you succeed, which could mean to survive!

Often, you don't remember your dreams until later. Here is a prophetic example that happened to me.

Gabby Giffords

Living in Tucson, Arizona, we were supporters of Gabby Giffords, Arizona's representative in Congress. We donated one of our office desks to help her during her initial campaign for office. My wife sat next to Gabby when she was flying back to Tucson, and Giffords promised to get together soon. Shortly after that, Gabby announced her "Congress on the Corner." My wife and I made plans to attend, and we were to meet my wife's mother at the event.

That morning, we had breakfast at the local restaurant we occasionally visited. After breakfast, we always drove north for 3 miles and then turned west for another 2 miles to get to our office. At the intersection where we would have turned west was the Safeway supermarket, where the meeting was being held.

But for an unknown reason, as I drove towards my usual exit that would take us towards the meeting, I drove around the restaurant to a different exit. My wife asked me why I was circling the restaurant and I could only answer, "I don't know." When I got onto the road, I could still get into the right lane that would head directly to the Safeway supermarket. I just had a feeling that I should "go straight," so I did. I drove west and then north to our office, totally avoiding the Safeway supermarket.

In our office, we began hearing many sirens from the nearby hospital and wondered what was happening. We found out when my wife got a call from her mother, who was to join us at the meeting. She was frantically crying and was so relieved to hear my wife's voice. A friend's phone call had delayed her that morning. As she drove to the supermarket, she found the area completely blocked off. She thought we were at the meeting and may have been killed. The assailant shot Gabby in the head, which left her severely handicapped. He shot 18 others, of which 6 died.

We gained further insight into the shooting when we went back to the same restaurant the following weekend. The server who knew us asked if we remember the gentleman who paid and left just before we did. My wife sort of remembered that he was an older man. The server said he and his wife went directly to the meeting with Gabby and he was the man killed protecting his wife.

So why did we both forget we had planned to attend the meeting with Gabby that morning? And what caused me to avoid the usual exit and then have a feeling to drive west instead of north to get to our office? I believe my dreams had warned me, and I later sensed the instruction to drive in a different direction.

You as a Psychic

Is there any area of your life that you would like to have a glimpse of the future? Think about it for a second. I'll leave this up to you to see if an insight into your future could be beneficial. There are several factors to consider when having a psychic dream:

- **Timing:** It's very difficult, if not impossible, to know the exact time the event you've seen will take place.

- **Qualities of the Dream:** Psychic dreams have 3 qualities. They are real, emotional, and vivid. If the dream has these three qualities, it's likely a psychic one.

- **Shared Dream:** There's also a chance that having the above three qualities, the dream is a shared dream.

When discussing a psychic dream, many people will say it's your imagination or you're a fool. If you're skeptical, keep an open mind. Be observant and you may see how often your dreams are depicting emotional or significant events in your dreams or the dreams of loved ones.

Chapter 12
Miscellaneous Success Dreams

I've included the following examples to show you the wide range of dream possibilities. If you're into sports, could your dreams help you improve as they did for Jack Nicklaus? While you won't be freeing a nation as Mahatma Gandhi did, but Martin Luther King Jr. had a dream and inspired change in the United States. The message you had in last night's dream or nightmare may surprise you with what it was saying to you.

Miscellaneous Examples

- **Bible:** Biblical figures believed their dreams or visions were instructions from God. Dreams were divine communication and should be just as valid now as it was back then.

- **Carl Jung:** Jung believed people could access the collective mind of humanity through a person's dreams. He studied dream interpretation and recorded his dreams.

- **Hannibal:** A military genius who used his dreams to create his battle plans. His dream told him to invade Italy and even gave him the idea of using elephants. While many of the animals died crossing the Alps, those that survived panicked the Roman cavalry and their Gallic Allies.

- **Jack Nicklaus:** As a professional golfer, Nicklaus had been playing poorly for two days. He then had a dream where he was hitting the ball very well. Looking down, he realized he was not holding the club as he had been lately. The next morning, he changed his grip to the one in his dream and shot 68 and then 65 on the following day. For those who are not golfers, those are excellent scores.

- **Clive Barker:** Barker, an author, director, and painter, keeps a dream journal of images and ideas. He then waits for additional inspirational input that pulls the original pieces together.

- **Mahatma Gandhi:** Gandhi protested the Rowlatt Acts which limited the civil liberties of Indians in the name of preventing terrorist violence. The legislature rejected his protests. Gandhi then had a dream where the country should go on a hunger strike. The entire country went on a hunger strike for a day of fasting and prayer. This started the nonviolent campaign against British rule and ended with India's independence.

- **Lester Jennings Hendershot:** Hendershot had a dream of how to create a fuel-less motor that would operate on "Earth currents." He fabricated the motor from an old radio and used it to fly a small airplane that his son had built. If you don't think this is fantastic, think about any object that could fly with no source of power.

- **Roman Emperor Caligula:** His dream found him standing before the throne of Jupiter. Jupiter, the king of the gods and god of the sky and thunder in Roman mythology, rejected him and kicked him back down to Earth. Although it showed his death, Caligula ignored the dream, and a conspiracy assassinated him the next day.

Hunches and Feelings

Have you ever had a feeling that you should try something different? Were you ever planning to do something and suddenly change your mind? When I bought a lottery ticket based on a feeling and won, it serves as an example. The above example of not driving the usual route to our office after breakfast is another.

So if you take a different route for no real reason, it could be one of those moments that's preventing an accident or guiding you somewhere. Hitting a series of red lights may do the same thing. You may not realize that you missed being in an accident by changing your route or being delayed by red lights. So there's no need to justify your changes other than to say, "I just felt like doing this," or "I just thought this may be better," or even, "I don't know."

I've included some examples of what has happened to me to show what you can do. Look at it this way; if I can do it, so can you. I've been able to transform my life, and it's my purpose to help you improve yours. I'm sharing what I know about being creative and innovative, so hopefully, you're motivated to see what's possible in line with your background.

Chapter 13
Developing a Creative Mindset

Dreams are today's answers to tomorrow's questions.
— Edgar Cayce

Creativity and innovation are directly related. Innovation is the use of a creative idea on a practical project, such as finding a better solution to a customer's problem. Building a faster fulfillment system is creativity in action. So we'll focus this chapter on becoming more creative and innovative. We'll begin by understanding how the mind operates. You'll also see how your thoughts are detrimental to having and maintaining a creative mindset.

The Creative Organization

You can apply and use creativity in all areas of your work or professional life. From ideas for starting a new business to building a new manufacturing plant, creativity allows you to go beyond your present (and often limited) mindset. In today's rapidly changing and evolving environment, everything is quickly becoming obsolete or passé. What you see around you is quickly being replaced.

In business, your competitors are inevitably working on developing new products and services that are leapfrogging the best the world offers. It's not good enough to copy the competition. While you're copying them, they're creating the next leap forward. If you're not creatively leading the way, customers will see you as a second-tier organization that's struggling to keep up with the best.

To excel, you need a set of tools that enables you to create and offer unique products and services. All real and perceived improvements add value to the products and services you offer. Otherwise, your competitors will quickly move in, push you aside, and steal your market share.

Creativity and You

You're already creative. You've been practicing creativity in small and large ways all of your life. If you did any of the following, you're showing your creativity:

- Drew a picture that no one understood.
- Shot a photo and improve the result by using different angles.
- Moved the furniture in a room to make it feel more like you.

Creativity at Work

There are 6 areas of work where you can apply creativity. Purists would say that they primarily consider the first five as innovation. Each of these will either improve performance or increase productivity. Which of these is the best candidate for you to work on right now?

- **Do More:** produce more results in the same period.
- **Do It with Less:** discover a way to accomplish the same results using less material and/or human resources.
- **Do It Faster:** respond and complete the job quickly. Not just working harder and faster, but eliminating unnecessary steps and paperwork.
- **Do It Cheaper:** lower costs and expenses without lowering quality.
- **Do It Better:** improve or create the perception that you have improved your product and services. The higher the perceived value, the higher price it commands.
- **Do It Differently:** different is where creativity shines. You have the chance to leap to another level of product or service.

Which of the above is an area you wish to work in? If you can accomplish 2 or more of these through the same creative effort, you'll make a more powerful improvement in productivity.

It doesn't matter if you're in management, sales, marketing, production, design, administration, or accounting. The improvement results will go straight to the bottom line. There's an improvement opportunity in every position in any organization. Improvement is no longer optional. Your customers are looking for the latest and greatest. That translates to more for less, faster, cheaper, better, and/or different. After all, when you're buying anything, aren't you looking at these factors?

Fortunately, you already possess the talent and ability to become more creative. You can slip beyond your current mindset and unleash your creative potential. However, creativity is not the process commonly referred to as "creative thinking."

All forms of thinking restrict you from going beyond your present paradigms or beliefs. All efforts with creative thinking will usually fail. The key limitation is in the word "thinking." All thinking is a simple process that's static. True creativity and innovation come from your ability to go beyond thinking. They credit Albert Einstein with saying, "Problems cannot be solved on the same level of mind that created them." Before you try to go beyond thinking, you need to understand the actual processes involved when you think.

The Thinking Process

Thinking is a simple and repetitive process that involves 3 basic processes. These functional processes are logic, reason, and memory. When you understand the basic interaction among these three, you'll realize how you think and the limitations within the process. You'll then be ready to leave the limits of thinking behind and shift your mind into a more creative mode.

Logic

The first basic tool in thinking is the use of logic. Logic is a collection of basic rules of how you should think if you're to remain logical. Philosophers have created these rules and many more special condition rules. Together, the rules governing how we should think if we were to think and communicate logically.

There's no need to go in-depth into these rules. It's enough that you realize these rules govern logical thinking. When you can't follow these rules, you are not being logical.

A simple example of one of these rules goes like this:

If A, then B,

A, therefore B

In a real-life example, it would read, "If it rains, then we won't have a picnic. It's raining; therefore, we won't have a picnic." You'll accept this as a perfectly logical statement.

But if we changed the statement, so it reads, "If it rains, then we won't have a picnic. It's raining; therefore, we'll still have the picnic." You would immediately reject this as a false statement. You'd criticize the person who made that statement as being illogical or even stupid.

Logic is the application of the rules of logic, repeatedly. As long as you communicate in a manner that follows these rules, people will regard you as a logical person. There's nothing creative or innovative about being logical and following the rules of logic.

To be creative, you need to go beyond the rules of logic. You may have to discover something illogical, something that doesn't yet exist. Fifty years ago, a driverless car would seem illogical. You would have said the same thing about virtual surgery or a robot giving a speech to a trade association convention. Creative people who will break the rules of logic will create tomorrow. However, if you break too many rules for no good reason, people will consider you as being artistic or crazy.

Reason

Reason is the second tool of thinking. It limits what you'll accept based on what you believe is possible or true. If a statement runs up against the limits you've set for yourself or limits set by some authority you respected, you'll question the validity of the statement. If a statement goes much beyond those limits, you'll almost automatically reject that statement. You'll say the statement wasn't "reasonable." You'll even do this when the statement proves to be completely logical. The following is an example I've used in one of my presentations.

> *I'll ask one attendee, "Suppose you were very thirsty. How long would it take you to drink a regular glass of water?" The usual answer is "about a minute."*
>
> *I then say, "Logic says that if you can drink a glass of water in about a minute, it means you can drink two glasses in two minutes."*

The audience usually "gets" where I'm going with this point and begins to giggle and laugh. I continue with,

"Following the rules of logic, I can conclude that you can drink 60 glasses of water in an hour and 120 in two hours. Do you agree you can do this?"

This is when the person's reasoning kicks in and rejects my statement. Even though this statement is perfectly logical, they realize that this isn't possible. They may recall how difficult a time they had drinking even eight glasses of water in a day. They intuitively know that drinking 60 glasses of water in an hour is impossible for them to do.

Your ability to reason is a valuable tool for identifying what goes beyond your acceptable limits. It's like a safety switch that rejects things that are beyond what your experience or imagined experience will accept. It also rejects what you believe to be false or impossible, despite being logical. For instance, if you believe carbon dioxide emissions from fossil fuels cause global warming; you'll not entertain any other cause of global warming. You'll automatically reject any arguments to the contrary, including gas from cows, horses, and vegetarians. You'll also reject the ideas that increased solar activity, forest fires, or more volcanic eruptions cause global warming. It doesn't matter that the argument is factual and logical; you may still consider the source to be ignorant or just plain stupid. At that point, realize that you're stuck in your current paradigms or beliefs.

People trap themselves with their personal beliefs or paradigms. Their common paradigms deal with age, wealth, race, and sex. They also have education, beauty, exercise, smartphone, automobiles, and vacation paradigms. The worst are political and religious paradigms. Finally, some people will hurt themselves and even die on their food and diet paradigms.

In the same way, your reasonable limits could easily reject a workable, new, and creative idea. Starbucks initially rejected the idea of cold coffee drinks because it was outside their paradigm of serving hot coffee. To tap your creative level of mind, be willing to put aside being reasonable. You should be open to those "far out" ideas that a reasonable person would never consider or would have outright rejected. Forget about your safety net of "who else is doing it?" Be willing to take a risk to be the first or an outlier.

If I had asked people what they wanted, they would have said, faster horses. — Henry Ford

Memory

The last tool of thinking is the ability to recall information previously gathered. You can only remember the information you've already collected. If you didn't already have some specific bits of information, it'd be impossible for you to recall it.

You can easily recall your name and birthday and even remember complex ideas and solutions you've learned in school or at work. What you can't recall is something you never stored in your memory, such as the address of my first home.

That's the first problem with my memory and yours. Like the computer, what you put in should be what you get out. If you put garbage in, you'll get garbage out. If you put in excellent information, then that's what you'll get out in the future. But if you have nothing in memory, you have nothing to recall.

There's another problem with memory. You may not find the memory you're searching for. Your memory may have forgotten things or become distorted with time. You may combine memories and create new memories. Or you may now believe the exact opposite of what you originally stored in your memory.

You could look it up on the Internet, but you have no assurance the information is correct. What you find may be false or outdated. You may simply reject correct information based on your beliefs, prejudices, fears, and desires.

You're probably thinking that this isn't correct. After all, you can use things in your memory and combine them to make something unique and creative. That's true. You'll see that combining ideas you know is preparation for your dreams to kick it up another notch. You'll see it discussed in a later chapter. For now, you only need to know that your memory, along with logic and reason, can't be creative.

Preparation

The Right Sleep Environment

To get the best results, I recommend you create the right sleep environment:

- Minimize all sources of light.

- Control any early morning disturbances, such as pets and children.

- Set room temperature to a cool setting (if possible).

- Minimize all sources of noise, such as alarm clocks, radios, and television. Try waking up without an alarm. If work makes this impossible, try it on weekends or your days off.

- Have a tiny and discreet light source that you can turn on with little effort.

- Have a pad and pen or pencil. There are pens with a light source built into the pen.

- If you're using a voice recorder, practice turning the recorder on and off with your eyes closed. Practice this until you can "do it in your sleep.

Right Attitude

As you head off to bed, you need to let go of any stress, emotions, anger, and fears. The following will help you calm yourself:

- Minimize stress by reviewing all the incidents during the day and forgiving the other party. Then forgive yourself for your part in the incidents.

- Have a positive expectation that your dreams will give you what you desire. If you can't get it on your first try, keep repeating the process.

Business Sense

To be creative in any field, have a good working knowledge of what you wish to work on. To become a creative author, you need to at least be knowledgeable on a topic you wish to write about. If you wish to create a new business, you need a working knowledge of running a business and also the product or service the public wants, needs, or demands. Of course, you may provide a product that no one has yet realized it's a product they need. It would be an unarticulated need, such as Facebook and Airbnb was.

A close friend of mine wants to start a mini-brewery. He's been experimenting with creating beers as a hobby for the past 20 years. He's getting a degree in beer brewing and then plans to expand his skills by working in a mini-brewery. Only then does he feel he's ready to open his mini-brewery. Meanwhile, he can use his dreams to gain special insights. They can give him new ideas to create and test, possibly creating the next "hot" cold one or brew. Other dreams may guide him to create an environment that will appeal to and build a strong clientele. He may even expand his dream to become the next "Star-brew."

Taking Action

To inspire you to continue, here are a couple of people who received dream insights and ran with them.

- **Dennis Quaid's wife, Kimberly**, awoke feeling her newborn twins were in danger. Quaid called the hospital and was told they were fine. They were not! Kimberly went to the hospital and found the babies were each given a massive overdose of anti-clotting drugs. The twins spent 11 days in intensive care before recovering. Kimberly's dream feelings were more accurate than the medical staff at the hospital.

- **J. Connon Middleton** had booked passage on the Titanic. A few days later, his dream showed the ship with its keel up with passengers and crew swimming around her. The dream repeated itself, and Middleton still did not cancel his booking. But life intervened, and he was told to delay his trip for business reasons. You may read whatever you wish into this story, but in your dream state, the possibilities are endless.

Sometimes, you're not aware of your dream messages. However, when you have a quiet moment to yourself, you may get the message in a feeling or sense that something is wrong or a feeling to do something differently. A Wall Street executive had a powerful message on his way to work.

- In 1993, Wall Street executive **Barrett Naylor** rode the train to work and had a premonition about the World Trade Center. This powerful feeling told him he had to return home. He reluctantly did and missed the bombing in the building's basement that morning. Eight years later, Naylor had the same feeling of dread on the train. He returned home in time to see the Twin Towers burning on TV. Again, Naylor acted on his premonition.

This happened to me when my wife and I were going to Gabby Gifford's "Congress on the Corner." The key is to pay attention and evaluate what your feelings and senses are trying to tell you. Naturally, never be foolhardy and place yourself when a mistake could cost you your life. Nor should you give anyone else any advice that may endanger them or even make them look foolish.

Chapter 14
Get the Dreams You Want

Whatever you do, or dream you can, begin it. Boldness has genius and power and magic in it

— Goethe

In a study, Dr. Deirdre Barrett of Harvard Medical School had her students focus on an unsolved problem they had before they fell asleep. They did this every night for a week. Two-thirds of her students found their dreams addressed the problem they had. One-third of them reported they received a solution to their problem.

Programming Your Dreams

A program is a simple statement of what you desire. You say it out loud and then go to sleep. If you wish, you could say it with more energy and emotions, but it's unnecessary.

Programming for a Creative Idea

Just before going to sleep, repeat:

> *I've been working on discovering a creative idea about _____. I need a great idea that will help me to _____. When I get up in the morning, I'll remember my dreams and be able to use them to make progress. I know that all of my efforts will be supported.*

Then go to sleep. The dream you remember the next morning may provide you with a creative idea. Immediately record it in your dream journal or record it into your recorder. Then, start working on this new idea. Your subconscious mind will know if you followed through or ignored the message. If you don't follow through, it may be a while before you receive another significant dream.

Programming my dreams for creative ideas gave me different approaches to my speeches. It helped me to develop effective methods to test the critical components in the Poseidon nuclear warheads.

If the programming doesn't work the first time, don't get discouraged. Your inner intelligence notes all of your efforts. Nothing positive ever goes unrewarded. You'll receive an appropriate reward for all the good you've done in your life and more. With dreams, all positive efforts will guide you to achieve the results you desire.

Programming for Innovative Solutions

Just before going to sleep, repeat:

> I've been working on discovering an innovative solution for _____. I need a brilliant solution that will help me to _____. When I am awake, I'll remember my dreams and be able to use them to make progress. I know that all of my efforts will be supported.

Again, go directly to bed and go to sleep. Don't get distracted by something undone or head to the bathroom one more time.

Example of an Innovative Solution

A few days ago, as I was writing this book, my computer had a few problems. Some apps worked and others didn't. I tried repairing all the problem software, and it didn't help. Since this was a new computer, I thought of removing all my programs and files and returning the computer to the store the next morning. But before I did that, I confidently told my wife that I would use my dreams to solve the problem.

The next morning, I remembered my dream. I went directly to the computer and fixed the problem.

When my wife asked if my dreams gave me the solution, I told her it did! My dream found me in a silent place where there was nothing but snow everywhere. Suddenly, lava erupted from the ground and melted all the snow as the lava covered the ground. The ground was now cool and plants were growing out of the lava.

I told her, "The dream meant that the software I was using was corrupted and had to be completely removed from my computer. I knew I had to reinstall the program. After I did that, that program and others worked fine."

"How did you know that the snow and lava dream was telling you how to fix your computer?" she asked.

"Because I programmed my dreams to solve my computer problem before I fell asleep. I saw the white snow showing the computer program environment was cold and dead. I realized the lava was replacing the old program with a new one. Then, the plants showed the program would work again."

Can it be that simple? Yep! But remember, I've been analyzing my dreams for decades. With a little experience, you can become just as proficient. It just takes a little practice and a belief that you can do it.

Ask better questions; then your dreams can provide better answers.

— Gary K. Yamamoto

Programming for Relationship, Love, and Sex

People have had sex dreams as long as there have been humans. The dream stories I have heard range from over-the-top fantastic to how difficult and clumsy it was. Some dreams were comedies, while others were sensual and romantic.

For most people, their sex dreams were a chance occurrence. But now that you're aware that you can program yourself to have the dreams you desire, it's time to take advantage of it. So the question is simple—what are you looking for that your dreams can help you find?

If you're looking for a long-term and meaningful relationship, you can program your dreams to help you find your soulmate. If you're just looking for someone to be a friend or perhaps a travel companion, that's also possible. And if you're searching for love with a wild and adventurous relationship, ask for it in a dream and see what happens. It's not only possible; it's a very doable thing.

Your dreams may guide you to find a person who is there for a short-time relationship. You may even get married, but after completing the shared experience, divorce may be the next best step. It's okay. After all, I'm a priest and I don't believe marriage must last until you die. Marriages should last as long as you love and remain supportive of each other. Otherwise, your marriage is living a lie, something that you tolerate or suffer. Your dreams can offer wise counsel. After all, it's your inner intelligence giving you advice that's best for you.

Use the following to discover and understand a relationship.

> *I've been working on finding an excellent relationship. I would like to experience what this person is like and see how compatible we will be. The primary object of this dream is to _____. When I get up in the morning, I'll remember my experience with this person and understand our compatibility. I know all my efforts will be supported.*

You can use the above programming statement and substitute the following phrases to have the dream of your choice:

- Travel companion.
- Future spouse.
- Soul mate.
- Love interest.
- Great lover.
- Memorable sex.

Another way to use your dreams is to meet someone for a wonderful romantic evening or even a simple wild party on the beach. Remember, these are your dreams and you are the master in your dreams. The possibilities are endless, as unlimited as your imagination. Wherever you want to go and whatever you wish to do, your dreams can take you there.

NOTE: if you have a low self-image or poor self-esteem, it may subconsciously alter the dreams you have. It's important that you feel good about yourself.

Have you ever fantasized about having a sexual rendezvous with a movie star or the person in your dreams? It's possible! You just program yourself to have that dream and it could happen. Of course, I know what you may be thinking. Perhaps you may think you're not good enough. You're not as good-looking as a movie star and the person may reject you. But remember, this is your dream. You can be whoever you wish to be. You can transform your face and physique to be even better than any plastic surgeon could create. There are no limits on who you could be or what you can do. In your dreams, you've left the old self behind and can be the person you always wanted to be.

This covert encounter could be anywhere you desire. It could be a part of an adventure or on a secret island in the middle of the ocean. If you think this is all so far out, put your doubts aside. I have had people sharing their dreams that would make a wonderful and sensual novel. You don't know what dreams you could have and what the future may hold because of it. I've heard a couple of dreams where the sexual dreams resulted in them finding their future spouse. People have related that their sex dreams were the most intense dreams they have ever had. The dream was so real that they weren't sure if it was a dream or if it actually happened.

Of course, there are those out there who would criticize you for doing this. They may call you names and say you've gone over the edge. But you don't have to explain your dream life to anyone. It can be your secret, a life of adventure and fun.

Rex Havens is a humorist speaker on marriage who makes fun of sex dreams. As part of his routine, he says his wife gets up in the morning and hits him, saying, "You know what you were doing in my dream?"

Programming for an Answer to a Question

> *I've been working on finding an answer to a question? I need a brilliant, yet practical, answer to help me to/with _____. When I wake up, I'll remember my dreams and be able to use them to improve my relationship and my life. I know that all of my efforts will be supported.*

Again, go directly to bed and go to sleep. Don't get distracted by something undone or head to the bathroom one more time.

When someone asks my opinion on what they should do, I often tell them to ask about their dreams. After all, their dreams can offer the best advice. Most of the time, the questions involve making one of two choices. It's very rare, but when there are over 2 choices, your dreams offer the best solutions. You could do this when people ask you for advice.

Therefore, refrain from giving advice. In almost all cases, you only know the questioner's point of view. You don't have the full picture. So when you say something that the person asking doesn't like, they will come back with a statement, such as,

"Yes, but… there's this and that and…"

"Yeah, but what about…"

If you're not a professional psychic and are not fully aware of the situation, your best advice is to tell the questioner to use their dreams to find the best solution.

What About Children: Of course, if it's your children who are asking the questions, then you must decide how to answer their questions. If you tell them to listen to their dreams, the answers they receive may surprise or even shock you.

Hypnagogia and Hypnopompic

Hypnagogia is the state we experience as we fall asleep. This state is the interval between being awake and being asleep. It's when your brain is aware enough that it can know what's happening as you fall out of a conscious state into a sleeping one.

Hypnopompic occurs when we're getting up after being asleep. Your brain is becoming aware and gets to a state of becoming conscious. It's at that point that your mind realizes the ending of a dream state. It can recall the details of the dream and can recall enough to record it. Using a miniature recorder is very useful here. But a simple pen and paper will also do the job.

As you wake in the morning, being aware makes it possible to enter a lucid dreaming state. If you can maintain your conscious state as you fall back asleep, you'll realize that you're awake in the middle of a dream. You can experience the possibilities in a lucid dream.

In either state, your mind is not attached to its normal beliefs, fears, and limitations. Instead, it's wide open to possibilities, even ideas that your conscious mind would ridicule or reject. These states make it possible to more fully realize the messages and insights found in your dreams.

There are reports of how some renowned artists and inventors have had their great insights when they were in these states. An example is the ball bearings and pan that Thomas Edison used to bring him out from entering a dream state. It's also the methods reportedly used by Nikola Tesla to get his ideas, including the one for alternating current and the phase syncing of generators.

Application

To take advantage of these states, do:

- Have a pen and paper next to your bed.
- Before falling asleep, think of what you wish to know or work on or program yourself.
- Observe, with little thought, allowing images or words to form.
- Record what you recall.
- When waking up, take your time and recall your dream.
- When any thoughts, solutions, ideas, etc. form, record them.

When fully awake, contemplate on what you recorded. It may be what you need right now or what you may find useful soon. Never discard your dreams; it's a good practice to review them periodically. You may see an idea or solution that may be useful at a later date or on a different project. Many have reported having visions, prophetic insights, solutions, and other useful realizations.

Final Note on Programming Your Dreams

You'll find examples of the time it may take to fulfill a dream prediction in the Lottery winner's examples. Some dreamers received their lottery numbers and won almost immediately. Others got their numbers and took as long as a couple of decades to win. What they had in common was they didn't give up on the dream. But as I mentioned before, don't spend money on the lottery that you can't afford to lose it.

Contemplation

Once you have your dream, it's important to contemplate on the dream. It may not hit you immediately. But sitting there and thinking how the dream may apply to the situation or problem you're working on, a clearer understanding or meaning may come to you.

If you've been asking for an answer or idea over several nights, you could look at what you've recorded in your dream logbook. By reading them together, it could trigger an insight you've missed before. Or it could help you create your next dream that could provide what you need.

Although a lot of the examples given in this book failed to show how long it took to get the dreams they used, you can be sure it wasn't always the very next morning. It could take a few days. Of course, it took Richard Bach 7 years and two lottery winners many more years.

The key here is to never lose faith and give up. Keep on programming your dreams and recording what you receive when you wake up. As a side observation, there are those who wake in the morning with multiple dreams. One woman said she gets up in the morning recalling 7 separate dream sessions. She said she could write a short story about each dream. Imagine having perfect really of every dream you have each night and trying to analyze them. Recalling one dream each morning may be sufficient for you.

Chapter 15
Your Dream Log

You're ready to record your dreams. That should be easy enough. It's been my experience that many people don't remember their dreams. Unless you're one of those who has this problem, the following recommendation may help:

- **Get Sufficient Sleep:** There's no real standard for the proper amount of sleep. But if you repeatedly yawn during the day and feel tired without really exerting yourself, that's a sure sign you need more sleep.

- **Wake up Naturally:** On weekends or days off, allow yourself to wake up without an alarm. Immediately record any dream you remember.

- **Program Your Wake Up:** Set your wake-up time by saying that's when you will get up. Tell yourself you will get up at 7 am and your inner clock will wake you. When your eyes open, please don't close them again and fall back asleep.

- **Avoid Drugs:** Don't use any sleeping pills, tranquilizers, or alcohol before going to bed. These drugs can render you unconscious and impede your ability to recall your dreams.

No Dream Recall

But suppose you receive enough sleep but still can't recall your dreams. A psychological block may prevent recalls. Here's a method that has proven successful with many people.

- Get a glass of water just before going to bed.

- Be sure it has a cover. It's disturbing to find that something has shared your water during the night and is now floating on top or swimming in it.

- Say out loud, "I will drink half of the water now, to prepare me to remember my dreams. In the morning, when I drink the rest of this water, I will remember my dreams.

- Drink half the water in the glass. Put the cover on the glass and set it in some convenient place near your bed.

- Go to sleep.

- When waking the next morning and recalling a dream, please write it down. (You can skip the next three steps).

- If you don't recall a dream, say out loud with emotion, "Upon drinking this glass of water, I will remember my dreams!.

- Drink the rest of the water.

- If you recall a dream, write it down. If not, be ready to record it if you remember it later in the day.

If this doesn't happen at first, don't give up. You may occasionally require nightly repetition. With so much to gain through dream recollection and analysis, your efforts are worthwhile.

A Dream Assistant

There is one method of dream recall that won't fail:

- **An Assistant:** Find a volunteer to assist you by staying up and watching you while you sleep. You can offer to trade this act with a friend or partner who is also interested in learning from their dreams. Your assistant wakes you right after you have completed a dream.

- **Rapid Eye Movement:** They'll know when to wake you by watching your eyelids twitching (Rapid Eye Movement or REM), which almost always accompanies a dream. When the REM stops, your assistant should gently awaken you.

- **Record Your Dream:** As you remember your dream, your assistant writes it down.

- **Assistant's Help:** Your assistant can further help by questioning you and writing what you recall.

Naturally, you should not use this method nightly. Being awakened right after a dream can interfere with your sleep, and you may not get the rest you need. If you get angry at the person for waking you, stop using this method.

Occasionally, you may recall a dream later in the day. You must stop whatever you're doing long enough to record it—even if you're in the middle of a shower. If you're driving, pull over and record your dream or speak it to your smartphone. This is especially important if you're remembering your first dream after years of minimal recall. Unless you do this, your newly gained ability may fade away. This may make future attempts even more difficult because it's saying that you're not interested in your dreams.

Dream Journal

A dream journal is essential. It's a record of your dreams. It may take two or more dreams to piece together a complete answer. Remember when Dennis Hong recorded his dreams when he got up during the night? In the morning, he would study what he wrote in the night. He then recorded the ones he found useful on his computer. You could do the same. Your dreams may spread your solution or idea over a few days or weeks. Hopefully, you won't wait as long as Richard Bach to get the rest of his book. The reason for the separation may be stressful situations at work or in your personal life that are preventing your complete dream solution. Or maybe you just aren't ready to handle the answer or solution.

It's a good idea to keep a small pad or mini recorder with you. Whenever you recall a dream or have a creative idea or solution, write it down. Then follow up by seeing how you can implement the dream suggestions. If they seem useful, take action. Once you're working on your dream suggestions, you'll remember more dreams.

Recording Your Dreams

There are only a few things to mention here. You need to capture your dreams as soon as you wake up. Here are a few suggestions that work:

- **Pen or Pencil and Paper:** Have these next to your bed. The best accessory I've seen was a paper holder that has a clip at the top that holds a pen or pencil. When you remove the pen or pencil, a tiny light comes on to assist you in writing your dreams. Without that light, you'll be scribbling in the dark, writing over a previous line, and find it impossible to read what you wrote.

- **Pen with a Built-in Light:** Another idea is a pen that lights up whenever the pen point presses down on the paper.

- **Dream Journal:** Record your dreams in your dream journal. This will keep your dreams in chronological order and allow you to have an easy reference to the progress you've made.

- **Lay in Bed for a Moment:** If you don't recall a dream, lay in bed for a couple of minutes. You may recall your dream. If you recall a dream, write it down immediately. The only exception would be if bathroom pressures force you out of bed.

- **Consider a Mini Recorder:** If you have a problem writing your dreams, consider having a mini recorder next to your bed. You need to practice how to start the recording in the dark. Nothing fades your dreams away faster than struggling to find the record button and wondering if it's recording. Also, know how to turn off the recorder.

- **Record Your Feelings:** If you had any feelings during the dream, make a note of how you felt in the dream.

Idea or Solution

Did your dream give you the insight, idea, or solution you were searching for? If it did, wonderful! If not, you can try again.

Once the dream is in your dream journal, it's saved and you can analyze it later in the day. Or, you can look back over time and see if you have a useful idea or solution you can now use in your life.

Bringing an Idea into Form

It is now time to develop your ideas into a useful product or service. This is where most people fail. It's said that most good ideas, products, and solutions will die with the inventor. Or, you may see an ad and think, "I dreamed of doing that years ago."

Constant improvement is also where a lot of companies fail. They develop a great product or service. Without constant improvements, competitors will begin stealing market share.

The Swiss created the quartz movement, but Texas Instruments and Seiko brought it to market. The Germans created the internal combustion engine, but the Americans brought it to market on a mass production basis.

Transforming an idea into a marketable product may require tremendous dedication and financial backing. This is where many individuals and organizations give up. Sony produced the Walkman© only because of the dedication and belief of co-founder, Masaru Ibuka. It was Fred Smith's complete belief in his vision of Federal Express® that made it real. Michael Dell's company built only custom computers, exactly what the customer wanted.

The Next Business Success

Many mega corporations have tens of thousands of employees. They got there through dedicated leadership and a continuous stream of creative ideas. Yet, at some point, many gigantic businesses cannot introduce innovative products and services the public wants. Their solution is to buy out smaller businesses that have creative and innovative products and services.

Creating a new business may be a dream away. And no, it's not impossible. After all, many great creative products and services started with one or two people working alone in their basement or garage. Bill Gates and Paul Allen started Microsoft, while Larry Page and Serve Brin founded Alphabet (parent company of Google). Steve Jobs and Steve Wozniak created Apple. Jeff Bezos founded Amazon just as Elon Musk founded Tesla.

Perhaps your dreams will guide you to create a company to sell it to a large corporation. You may think this is impossible, but it has happened so many times before. Microsoft has bought over 200 companies for billions of dollars. Apple bought Seri, NeXT, and Beats Electronics. Google has bought over 200 companies. Disney bought Lucasfilm and Marvel Comics. Amazon bought Whole Foods Market, Zappos, and dozens of other companies. Facebook bought Instagram, WhatsApp, and Oculus VR. Could you be creating the next company available for takeover for a lot of money? Why not! It could be you.

Fortunately, becoming an artist or an author doesn't require a large financial resource and group dedication. Remember how Jasper Johns was struggling to become an artist until he dreamed of painting an enormous flag? After he painted his best-known piece, "Flag," his career took a gigantic leap forward.

You need an idea and dedicate the time and energy to dream and create your masterpieces. While an author requires additional help with editing, both fields require marketing and sales of your creations. Marketing and sales can be a lot more difficult than creating your work of art. Fortunately, your dreams are available to help you there.

Chapter 16
Extracting the Dream Messages

Dreams are often most profound when they seem the most crazy.
— Sigmund Freud

There are several ways for you to get the message you seek. From the previous examples, there are simple methods to get your solutions. Unfortunately, these solutions are not the simple ones that you can get from a dictionary. Begin by reading and contemplating your dreams. Some had their answers given to them, written on their mind or on sheets of paper. The rest had to spend the time to extract their dream message and apply it practically. Below, I summarized what you can do to extract the right dreams:

Preparation

- **Contemplation:** Contemplate on a problem of a situation before falling asleep. Expect to get an answer. Remember to keep paper and pen or a recorder next to your bed.

- **Programming:** Ask for the dream you wish to have. Expect to wake up with a dream that provides an answer or the solution to the situation at hand.

- **Short naps:** Your author uses this often. A quick nap allows a dream to work on your situation and provides you with a workable answer.

Waking Up with a Dream

- **Record the storyline:** Capture the idea of what's happening in your dream. When you look at what's written, it may not make sense. You can always ask for another dream.

- **Different:** Was there anything that's not normal in your dream? Whenever something is different, it may be a key to the answer or solution you've been seeking.

- **An unusual environment:** Did the dream find you in a church or in a cave? Where you were may be an important key to the message of the dream.

- **Short dream with little detail:** This very short dream may be a part of an important and longer message. It may take many nights of small dreams to bring the idea or solution to you.

An Important Dream

- **Nightmares:** Nightmares show the message is important. The scarier the nightmare, the more urgent it is for you to record and analyze the dream.

Contemplation

- **Taking a shower:** If you don't recall your dreams, it may result from a wake-up alarm or a bathroom call. However, your mind is silent in the shower, the idea or solution returns to you. When it happens, you need to be ready to record the message.

- **Driving to work:** This is another time when you're quiet and open to recalling a dream. If possible, don't play music or listen to an audio program. Be ready with a digital recorder. Don't use your phone because that's probably illegal to use while driving.

- **Contemplate the dream:** Stop doing and ask yourself, "what if…" What if you could do it? What if someone came to help you? What if you removed your limitations? Then wait for an answer. It may feel silly, but an answer often comes.

- **Illness:** When you're ill, your thoughts stop. It's possible to recall or receive a dream message. Please don't make yourself ill to test if this works.

A Psychic Dream

- **Identifying a Psychic Dream:** Psychic dreams have 3 qualities. They tend to be real, emotional, and vivid. If the dream has these three qualities, it's likely a psychic one. Or, it could be a shared dream.

- **Timing:** It's very difficult, if not impossible to know the exact time and place a psychic event in your dreams will take place.

- **Deity:** If a divine being helps you solve problems that would be wonderful. If a deity comes to you with expert knowledge, record it and contemplate on the message.

Timing

- **Patience:** It may take a series of dreams to get the complete message. The successful authors I met at my Canyon Ranch presentations described how their dreams gave them material so they could add color and authenticity to their novels.

When in Doubt

- **Just do it:** When your dream has provided a solution, others may not like the idea. Check to be sure it will hurt no one. Then, you should just do it. You can always apologize later.

Dream Stock Pickers

- **Walt Stover** of Arizona started a stock precognition group in 1998. The initial group was using the methods based on Edgar Cayce's readings. To become a member of the group, they would screen perspective members based on their accuracy for their dreams of picking the right stocks. In 2003, Stover's stock portfolio increased by 52 percent. The next year, the group had dreams showing which stock to invest in for a 400% increase. One member followed his dream and made a profit of over $1.5 million US. You can research the methods used by this group from the Edgar Cayce's readings. This information is available at the Association for Research and Enlightenment (ARE) in Virginia Beach, Virginia.

I didn't mention this group suggesting you join that group. Instead, you could consider creating your own group. With the Internet and videoconferencing software, you can create a national or even an international group. Have each person share their dream stock pick and when they purchased the stock. That way, the entire group can focus on certain stocks and see if there is enough support to purchase the stock. Of course, each member of the group makes their own decision on what and when to buy and sell.

Chapter 17
Building a Business from Your Dreams

We can talk about it, dream about it and dissect the fine print. In the end, only action satisfies our longing.
— Gina Greenlee

You've recorded a dream. Study it to see if it has some relationship to what you programmed or asked for? Even if it doesn't, write what you had asked for before this dream. The message may become clear in the future or when combined with another dream. Then repeat the process by asking for another dream. If it does the answer or solution you needed, that's fantastic! It's time to put this latest guidance into action.

Artists: You're ready to begin. When you recall your dream, take out your pad and sketch it. As you get more details in subsequent dreams, be sure to note this in your dream journal or on your sketch pad. At every step of the way, your dreams can provide you with more insights and additional guidance.

Authors: When you are working on your book, use your dreams to help you finish your book. If you're writing a novel, your dreams can provide you with the plot and the characters. As an author I met at Canyon Ranch said you could get details for your novel. It can make your novel come alive as it paints a vivid picture in the minds of your readers. Keep all of this in your journal.

If you're writing non-fiction, you can use your dreams to give you insights on how to best format your book. It could give you your book title or provide you with ideas on how to market your book. As you continue to record your dreams, it could even suggest a rearrangement of your chapters.

Everyone: Whatever you're doing or working with, ask yourself the following question:

- Is there a way to do more with less, faster, cheaper, and/or better?

- Can I make it simpler or easier to do?

So look at everything you do. Everything in your life becomes a candidate for improvement. Amazon killed the standard other corporations were saying, "It may take up to six weeks to receive your order." Google Maps on your phone eliminated unfolding maps while driving or hiking. Uber ended your having to guess when your ride will be arriving. Zoom removed the need to travel to business meetings. And the smartphone has become the Swiss Knife of today.

Contemplation, the Secret Key: Even if you don't remember a dream or recall one that seems unrelated, don't think it was a failure. Take the time and simply stare at your work. It seems easier for the artist or author. However, even an inventor or scientist should simple spend some time contemplating their work. It's often from contemplation that ideas and solutions spring into your head. I believe that these spring out of earlier dreams in the night or the dreams you failed to recall.

Starting Your Dream Business

Out of clutter, find simplicity. From discord, find harmony. In the middle of difficulty, lies opportunity. — Albert Einstein

The following process takes advantage of creative ideas and innovative solutions. If it's a large project, you may require others with expertise in different disciplines. If you're doing this alone, you need to go through each step by yourself. Keep in mind that you can use this process to improve your work or profession, or to start a business.

- Identify your purpose.
- Select a group.
- Create a supportive culture.
- Brainstorm for ideas.
- Ask dumb questions.
- Combining ideas.
- Happy accidents.
- Take action.

Let's see how you'll go through this process and how you can use your dreams to get a unique insight, a solution, or a creative idea.

Identifying Your Purpose

Most people have a warped view of a creative person. In business, we may see creative people as eccentric, strangely dressed people who stare into space and wait for a light bulb to flash over their heads. It flashes, they jump up and out spews an unusual design, a new product, or perhaps a new marketing idea. This form of creativity may work for Wolfgang Amadeus Mozart, but it's not workable in today's world. Even Richard Bach worked on his book for many years before a dream revealed the ending.

For creativity to be useful, you must focus your effort on improving a particular product or service. You start your innovative project by identifying exactly what you're going to improve. Are you trying to build a better coffee machine, streamline a healing service you offer, or build a new type of airplane?

Select a Group

For an artist or an author, creativity or innovation is best done alone. But in our increasingly complex business environment, creativity is most effectively achieved in a group or team setting. Even the old artistic masters, such as Michelangelo and Leonardo de Vinci, had assistants. But even for a simple project like writing a book, you could use people to help you. You could hire contractors who are knowledgeable in research, editing, marketing, website design, public speaking, online sales, and order fulfillment.

Members of the group should come from all disciplines involved with the final product or service. Each has their unique point of view to contribute. In a business, members may include representatives from engineering, marketing, sales, manufacturing, customer service, and human resources.

When selecting the members of the group, ask for volunteers. People required to take part are rarely very creative. From the volunteers, select those excited by the proposed project.

Limit the number of participants. The ideal number seems to fall between four to eight people. For a major project, it's more effective to form smaller groups to handle different aspects of the project. However, the central group will coordinate and compile all results. Keep in mind that the larger the group, the more critical for the organization to have a positive culture and effective communications channels.

Create a Supportive Culture

After you have the right group or team, begin by creating a supportive environment. Let members know they are free to make suggestions and exchange ideas. A supportive culture has the following attributes:

A safe feeling: People need to feel safe to propose ideas, even wild and strange ideas. The primary stumbling block to creativity and innovation is fear. The most common fears are looking foolish, receiving negative feedback, and/or rejection. Personal fears may prevent some members from saying anything far outside the box or within acceptable limits.

- **An open environment:** Have an open work area where people can meet, share ideas, and find solutions to problems.

- **Empowered to take action:** Allow people the freedom to offer suggestions and then to explore creative solutions. A sense of ownership lets people go the extra mile. When Tim Cook first started working at Apple, it shocked him to see what happens with a new idea. If the idea sounded good, Steve Jobs simply said, "Okay, do it." There were no studies, no surveys, and no reviews. People simply owned their ideas and ran with them.

- **The right mental state:** Maintaining a positive attitude, emotional control, and strong self-esteem goes a long way to support your creative efforts.

- **Humility:** Realize that neither you nor anyone else has all the right answers. It's best to accept all suggestions, especially dream or moonshot ideas.

- **A sense of wonder and play:** Children are most creative when playing. Help the group recapture that sense of play and fun that they once had as a child. Just don't let it get too far out of hand.

- **Cultural diversity:** This is a powerful asset when you're trying to discover a unique solution or approach. In a homogeneous culture, people think similarly and look for solutions and ideas from similar points of view. They see the same opportunities and obstacles. They'll probably suggest similar solutions for overcoming those obstacles. It often helps to have someone with a unique background to see the situation and offer a different point of view.

The evening before his speech, a speaker forgot the cufflinks for his French cuff shirt. It was late Sunday and the first two department stores had no cufflinks. The third also had no cufflinks, but the clerk asked the speaker what they were for. He said he needed them for his special shirt. The clerk asked, "Why don't you buy another shirt?"

- **Programming dreams:** Have attendees program their dreams to uncover ideas and insights. Some may consider this silly or useless. However, you can introduce it as a game to see who can have the most creative dream on the project. Having many dreamers working on solving a problem or developing a creative angle is often very fruitful.

If you're working alone, having the right mental state and attitude is powerful. Fear of failure, frustration, anger, and feeling inadequate will hold you back. Avoid blaming others or making excuses for little or no progress. Regularly use your dreams for help.

Brainstorm for Ideas

When you've established a creative environment, you're ready to create a brainstorm. Begin by selecting one area and asking people for ideas or potential solutions. When brainstorming for solutions, you need a storm. A storm grows if the first clouds (suggestions) in the sky can grow.

The group must consider all ideas. They should allow no criticism or negative comments. Albert Einstein said, "Imagination is more important than knowledge." While imagined ideas that have sprouted from a person's dreams may not be logical or reasonable, they deserve consideration.

As ideas are being generated, record everyone's ideas. Group these ideas into general categories, such as production, marketing, sales, and customer service. Keep reminding people that all ideas are good ideas, no matter how impractical they may sound. Every idea, even if it appears impossible to implement or use, may be the springboard or seed for another idea that may work.

Even if you're working alone, don't skip this step. Spend your time looking for new ideas and alternative ways of looking at the situation. You could do some research on the Internet, to see if it triggers any new ideas. You can always use your dreams for suggestions.

Keep recording until the group has temporarily exhausted all ideas. With these ideas before the group, select one area, and have everyone concentrate on it.

Expand on an Idea

Focus on one area and ask everyone for ideas and comments on those ideas. If someone identifies a problem with an idea, first acknowledge and record it, then continue finding other workable solutions. It allows the group to concentrate on the problem and prevents the session from becoming a nonproductive argument.

Again, record every new idea or solution and have it projected on the wall. Then have everyone build on each idea posted by asking the following questions:

Ask Dumb Questions

Have someone in the group ask any of the following questions:

- What if the rules were different?
- What if we could not fail?
- What if we had unlimited resources?
- What if we could overcome the impossible?
- What if (fill in the blank) were not true?

Record any ideas that may become possible. Remember, this isn't serious. You're operating within the context of your mental and group playground. Allow it to play out with some outrageous ideas.

Other dumb questions could be:

- Why are we doing this?
- What are we really trying to accomplish?
- Who would want to use this?
- Do people really need this?

- Wouldn't it be easier if?

- Wouldn't it be better if?

- Does the buyer even care about his specific aspect?

The answers to these questions might shock you, but they're very important. They're coming from a unique or different point of view. They may point you and your efforts in a different direction. Sometimes those who are closest to an idea have the most difficulty in seeing an obvious, different, or unusual possibility.

> *Success Doesn't Just Show Up. Dream Big. Reach High.*
> *Achieve More Today!* — Wesam Fawzi

Standard Plans Program

When I saw engineers redrawing the same equipment installation plans over and over, I asked, "Why are we doing this?" The answer was simple—this was John's design, and he wanted to say, "this is my installation plan and I created it." It didn't matter that he was redrawing the same plans. The only difference may have been a few of the connections he was using.

Then I had a dream that showed me putting all the plans I used into a book and making it a standard. So I simply started creating a book of plans showing all the useful configurations, so I didn't have to always redraw the same plans over and over.

Of course, it's said that you should allow others to take credit for an idea you created. But when your bosses take credit and collect a monetary reward for your idea, it can sting a little.

Combining Ideas

- Many years ago, **Masaru Ibuka**, co-founder of Sony, was walking through one of Sony's plants. The engineers in the portable tape recorder production section were proud to show him what he believed was their latest portable tape recorder. He commented on how wonderful it was to have such a small recorder. They apologized and said it could not record. There was no space to put in the recording electronics. Ibuka continued walking and came across the headset development unit. They were so proud to show him their latest headset, which was small, light, and provided wonderful sound reproduction. He congratulated them and asked them to talk to the people with the tape recorder that did not record. It was the birth of the Walkman.

- **Steve Jobs** took the idea of the Walkman and put it together with the latest electronics to create the iPod. He later combined the iPod with the flip-top phone and created the iPhone. He then combined the iPhone with the iMac and created the iPad. I'm not downplaying Jobs' accomplishments, but can you look at how easy it may be to combine things to create something truly wonderful.

Happy Accidents

- **Henry Round:** Back in 1906, Round noticed a yellowish light emitted when he applied 10 volts to a silicon carbide crystal. It wasn't until 1931 that researchers at Texas Instruments noticed that applying a voltage to gallium-arsenide diode emits infrared light. That year, General Electric patented the infrared LED. That led to the creation of the red LED, the yellow LED, and then the high intensity LED which are used to transmit data through fiber optics cables. Now, different colors of LED are common. When Henry Round just noticed the light being emitted, he did not know how it would lead to a tremendous breakthrough in creating efficient light with a multitude of uses.

- **Sir Alexander** Fleming: Fleming noticed that a contaminated Petri dish he had thrown away contained a mold that was dissolving all the surrounding bacteria. That mold contained an antibiotic that was later labeled penicillin.

- **Chef George Crum:** He received back a customer's fried potatoes, asking him to cut them thinner and fry them longer. Upset, he finally sliced the potatoes extremely thin and fried them until they were as hard as possible without burning them. To his surprise, the customers loved what he created. They called it potato chips.

- **Percy Spencer:** Spencer was an engineer who worked at Raytheon, was developing a new vacuum tube for a new radar unit. He noticed that the candy bar in his pocket melted during the experiments. He put dried corn kernels into the device and when they popped; he knew this was an alternative method to cook food. Raytheon created the first microwave oven, which they labeled the Raytheon Radarange.

- **Patsy Sherman:** She was a chemist at 3M when she dropped a gooey mixture onto her shoe. She later noticed that her shoe was dirty except for one spot. She looked back at what she was working on and found the compound his company called Scotchgard.

- **Spencer Silver:** A researcher at 3M, Silver created a sample of glue that hardly held anything. A colleague thought of using the glue to hold pieces of paper to mark the songs for his choir. Initial results were disappointing until he gave away free samples and 94% said they would buy the product. They then changed the name to Post-It Notes.

- **Canon engineer:** At Canon, an engineer accidentally placed a hot iron on a pen and noticed how the ink squirted out. That observation formed the idea for an ink-jet printer.

- **Harry Brearley:** He experimented with different metal compounds and discarded his failures. The discards quickly rusted, except for one. They changed the name from "rustless steel" to stainless steel.

- **Roy Plunkett:** Plunkett was to experiment with gas and left it overnight. In the morning, he found the gas had disappeared and left a slick material we now call Teflon.

- **George de Mestral:** He created Velcro when he looked at the burrs stuck in the fur of his dog under a microscope. It only gained worldwide use after astronauts began using it.

- **Charles Goodyear:** Goodyear invented vulcanized rubber when he accidentally dropped his rubber compound on top of a stove and noticed the changes that had taken place.

- **Physicist Wilhelm Roentgen:** Roentgen accidentally noticed the machine illuminated the fluorescent papers, even though the cover was on the machine. They called that process x-ray.

- **Edouard Benedictus:** He accidentally dropped a flask of glue onto a sheet of glass. After the glued had dried, it kept the glass from shattering, which resulted in the idea for safety glass.

These accidental inventions resulted from being aware and noticing what was happening. How many years have people found burrs on their clothing before George de Mestral used the idea to create Velcro?

When Spencer Silver accidentally created weak and reusable glue, he worked for over 5 years promoting the qualities of his glue. When an accident brings a possible creative idea to you, would you continue to promote it through your company and also give seminars on this glue? It was at one of Silver's seminars that an attendee thought of using it to mark their choir songbook.

You've probably exhausted everything you and the rest of the group can think of. You're now ready to go beyond thinking. Remember, exhausting all possibilities is important. If you can't do this, your thoughts will automatically search for answers through logic, reason, and memory. Only after it has tried everything, will it be ready to go beyond thinking into your creative mind. You do this by taking a break and waiting for an insight. You could always program your dreams for more insights and solutions.

Chapter 18
Your Dream Adventures

Each man should frame life so that at some future hours, fact and his dreaming meet.

— Victor Hugo

You have had dreams all your life. They were always there, doing want they do the best. They have one purpose—to help you succeed. On one level, they handle your everyday problems and situations. You may not have known that your dreams had significant messages for you. Most people only paid attention to their dreams if it had something to do with either money or sex. Otherwise, its just stuff that happens while they slept.

Rising Above

If you wish to rise above the masses, you need to pay attention to your dreams. Your normal dreams have a message for you that needs to be interpreted. To do that, I would recommend my other dream book, Creative Dream Analysis. It was specifically designed to help people understand their dream messages and improve their lives.

This book is for those who wish to get ahead with something different, something unique. We know that today's marketplace is flooded with goods and services. In order to excel, you must present something different. This is where your dreams excel. It allows you to move into another level, to find something different. The key is to program your dream to receive an idea or a solution.

Keep Going

The sure way of not progressing is to give up. When I worked on the cover for this book, my team and I went through several iterations. One person called me to say he dreamed the title of my book. It's the one on this book.

Authoring a book is a totally creative process. I revised the contents several times. I often woke up with a new angle or idea. For me, this was a powerful way to share what I had spent my whole life discovering. Dreams helped because I worked on 10 books at the same time.

Personal Validation

You'll realize the power of your dreams when you begin programming and recording your dreams. You may be shocked with what you receive. This is the challenge of life and the power of dreams.

My Wish

It my wish that you succeed in whatever field you with to enter and pursue. Your greatest success will be in the field that you are most interested in.

May you dream big dreams and accomplish even larger ones!

Supplement
History of Dream Analysis

People were aware of their dreams for thousands of years. They may have lacked the language or time and dimensions, but they knew their dreams were important. I've included this chapter to provide you with a glimpse of the evolution of dream analysis.

Dream analysis probably began when people realized their dreams and wondered what they were for. They looked at their lives and could see a correlation between the two. The following is the history of dreams and dream analysis:

- Over 12,000 years ago, the people in the mountains of India already used lucid dreaming to improve their lives and wellbeing.

- Around 5,000 BC, the Sumerians in Mesopotamia created the first book on dream symbols and their meaning. The Sumerians viewed dream symbols as signs given to them by their gods. They had dream priests who took a person's dreams and use them to foretell the person's future.

- Egyptians took the ideas from the Sumerians and viewed dreams as messages from their gods. They created their dream book. The Bishop Museum in London keeps a copy of that dream book in their archives.

- Over 2,000 years ago, Tibetan Buddhists used the technique of Dream Yoga to enter a lucid dreaming state. In that state, they would work on guiding people to better their lives.

- The Greeks were well aware of the power found in a person's dreams. Aristotle believed that sleep freed the mind of thoughts and memories of the activities of the day. Clarity made it possible for a person to achieve pure wisdom. Greek dream interpretation was used to increase and maintain the prosperity of the dreamer.

- While in Greece, I visited the site of the Oracle at Delphi. The Oracle was the principal source of wisdom for Greeks. Today, people aren't sure how the Oracle received her prophecies. Some claim she used drugs. Others believed the Oracle based her prophecies on her dreams and the dreams of her clients. A more recent idea is the gas that rose through earthquake faults put her into a dream-like state that allowed her to prophesize a person's future.

- The Bible talks about the power of being able to understand and interpret dreams. You can find passages on dreams in Genesis, Kings, Judges, Ecclesiastes, and Isaiah, and also in the New Testament.

- In 305 AD, Aristotle described lucid dreaming in his treatise "On Dreams." He believed that a person's consciousness was little more than a dream.

- The Romans then drew their dream knowledge from the Greeks. Caesar Augustus believed strongly in the prophetic nature of dreams. To unleash the dream power of all the people in his country; he created a law requiring a citizen to publicly discuss their dream in the marketplace.

- The Iroquois saw dreams as the language of the soul.

Back in 1985, I published my first dream book, *Creative Dream Analysis: A Guide to Self-Development*. I wanted to help people understand how to analyze the messages hidden in their ream. See more at:

www.creativedreamanalysis.com.

About the Author

I f you're interested in dreams, it's a big step to discover that the possibilities in your life are endless. We live in an almost magical appearing universe, filled with unlimited possibilities. Gary has spent his entire life discovering what's possible. He began the hard way, through books, teachers, seminars, and consultations. But he learned his greatest lessons when he lived alone in the middle of the desert. Except for a minimum of time at work, he spent the bulk of his time in meditation and prayer. The process lasted over 8 months, where he had his own spiritual experiences and revelations. He also learned that all of his earlier efforts were necessary; they prepared him to understand what he experienced. He wants to show people how to live independently and sanely in a world of conflict and extremes. Yes, it's possible.

- **Engineering:** Gary graduated from the University of Hawaii with a degree in electrical engineering. He discovered his dreams could help him pass exams.

- **Civil Servant:** Gary used his dreams to solve engineering problems for 22 years as a communication and nuclear weapons engineer.

- **Metaphysics:** He studied Reiki under Hawayo Takata, at one of her first classes in Hawaii. His studies also included reflexology, past life readings, meditation, group synergy, health and healing methods, channeling, massage therapy, meditation, energy transmission, dream interpretation, remote viewing, etc.

- **Instructor and Seminar Leader:** He taught dream interpretation and many other metaphysical topics beginning in the mid-1970s.

- **College Instructor:** He taught personal development and creativity classes at the University of Arizona and Pima College.

- **Catholic Priest:** Gary was ordained a Catholic Priest in the Malabar Rites by Archbishop Patriarch, Adrian Spruit.

- **Book Publisher:** Founded Harbinger House, a trade book publishing company.
- **Health Lecturer:** Gary has lectured for years on dreams and dream interpretation at the exclusive Canyon Ranch Spa in Tucson, Arizona.
- **Public Speaker:** Gary became a full-time public speaker for corporations, trade associations, and government agencies.
- **Business Owner:** Gary co-founded Gold Stars Speakers Bureau in 1989 and it's still in business after 30 years.
- **Author:** He is also the author of several books and audio programs.

Gary's desire is for you to learn to use and benefit from your dreams. Imagine you and your significant other using your dreams to transform your life. Or, you could start a dream group to help your investments. Your dreams could also trigger an idea to start a new business or improve an old one.

Dreamers indeed accomplish nothing. It's also true that those who work hard without dreams are simply living yesterday, all over again. But by paying attention to your dreams and acting on the ones that appear promising, you can unleash your energy and open your life to a world of possibilities!